CLES

T THIS

THE RAGLAN ROAD COOKBOOK

Inside America's Favorite Irish Pub

Kevin Dundon

MITCHELL BEAZLEY

RAGLAN ROAD
IRISH PUB AND RESTAURANT

An Hachette UK Company
www.hachette.co.uk

First published in 2014 by Inclined to be Inspired Ltd
This edition published in 2016 by Mitchell Beazley,
a division of Octopus Publishing Group Ltd
Carmelite House
50 Victoria Embankment
London EC4Y 0DZ
www.octopusbooks.co.uk
www.octopusbooksusa.com

Distributed in the US by
Hachette Book Group
1290 Avenue of the Americas
4th and 5th Floors
New York, NY 10020

Distributed in Canada by
Canadian Manda Group
664 Annette St.
Toronto, Ontario, Canada M6S 2C8

ISBN 978 1 78472 236 4

Printed and bound in China

10 9 8 7 6 5 4 3 2 1

Written by Neil Cubley & Kevin Dundon
Edited by Jennie Hess
Recipes by Kevin Dundon ©
Designed by Neworld Associates Ltd, Dublin, Ireland
Photography by Harry Weir, Ivan Cummings, Todd McCabe,
Harry Pidgeon, Paul Nolan. All copyrighted.

For

Soren, Saoirse and Connor O'Shea

Sharon Prior

and

Leslie Cooke

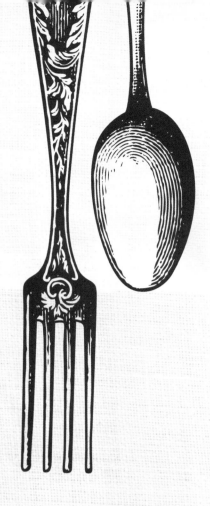

Contents

....

OF MICE AND IRISHMEN

Outside, it's 93 degrees with a similar dose of humidity – just
to be sure. If it ever got this hot in Ireland the Emerald Isle would
become Golden. Beyond, flocks of folks, young and old, follow their
dreams to the Kingdom.

Inside, Bill sits at the apex of the Grand Bar on his stool.
Bill owns this piece of real estate. He knows that this is the best
vantage point. Bill was the first to ever cross this threshold.
He gazes at the 140-year-old back bar and watches Vinny pour
yet another magical pint of Guinness. Beside him sit two new
friends from Vancouver. Two more friends added to a very long list.

Behind him, Danielle, in Irish dance garb, steps up on the
podium. The podium is 112 years old – a church pulpit in a former
life. She likes the fact that she can see her reflection in the antique
Irish wall mirrors left, right and centre. It helps her with her
moves. She flashes a brilliant smile at the fiddler in the band.
No Irishwoman ever had teeth this white. The fiddler – no slouch
in the gleaming-teeth department – flashes one back. Although a
novice in the marriage game, Colin knows better than to ignore
a loving gesture from his wife. He fires up the fiddle and, instantly,
the room begins to tap.

Bill Hazlett - First man at the bar

At the far bar – "Paddy's Bar" – two well-groomed folks order some scallops and a libation to wash them on their way. They are deep in discussion. They both nod knowingly at three others, ensconced across the Pub in the snug. They are all obviously of the same tribe. Each has a bulge in his or her pocket – a badge of some sort that has been removed prior to arriving. These people have the keys to the Kingdom but, right now, they are as tourists on foreign soil and, thus, off duty.

Behind this scene, Sean is fixing the automatic bread slicer which cost ten grand but won't slice bread. He's doing this whilst on his cell phone to his software support service discussing WiFi channels and frequencies and why neither seem to want to communicate with one another. "I can't get the router to sshhtaaartt," he repeats in his soft Kerry accent. His house earpiece crackles in his other ear as the podium host announces that "the table for 12 has arrived an hour early and, oh, the patio is full, and it's about to rain." Sean could have studied Business and International Languages instead when he entered University in Ireland. He mulls over this choice with some intensity.

And in the very far corner, three middle-aged Irishmen are seated in imported chairs. One is buried in an Excel sheet. One is besotted with Twitter. One is ending a phone conversation with L.A. All three have good hair and most of it their own.

Suddenly "L.A." sits forward and says "We should do a book! With millions of recipes. And a picture of me on the front cover." Twit is inspired by this. "It could be a brand expression, y'know, connect in a meaningful way and tell the true story of how Raglan came to be." Excel peers out over his glasses and then his laptop, sighs heavily and asks, if not for the first time – "And what's the margin?"

All three then sit back in their chairs, falling back into their little worlds, unconsciously agreeing that this was indeed another stupid idea.

Food

This book provides recipes for hearty creamy soups, savory stews, light salads, delicious desserts and much more. It covers the whole range of contemporary Irish cuisine, but it is also food that you can eat every day without hours of preparation. I have included past, present and future Raglan Road dishes. There are some absolutely brilliant dishes here that were on the menu then were removed because we simply didn't have room. Honestly, I had nearly forgotten some of these dishes over time, and I am delighted to introduce them to you!

It is important to me that the food in the book is all very accessible. There is nothing that will make you jump back and say, "I can't do that," because most cooks can make every dish at home. It might sound obvious but it is worth saying that every picture you see in this book is of a dish that I have personally cooked and then eaten afterward (and enjoyed!). The recipes would not be in here otherwise. You might be familiar with some cookbooks in which, even though you follow the recipe to the letter, your prepared dish looks nothing like the photo. Not here. What you see, you can create.

I have made sure that the steps are simple and very clear and that the recipes use ingredients that you should be able to find at a good local supermarket. There is nothing rare or obscure that you might struggle to find. Yes, there are some sophisticated dishes that take a bit more time, but that is as hard as it gets. And there are few of them. Remember, Irish cuisine, as it is eaten in Ireland today, is all about fresh ingredients, straightforward preparation and creative presentation. So go on—unleash your inner Irish!

Have fun cooking, and I hope to see you at Raglan Road again soon.

THE POET AND THE 'DUBLINER'

The Bailey, 1-4 Duke Street, Dublin 2, Ireland.
Patrick Kavanagh: Poet
Luke Kelly: Musician

One day, some time in the middle of the 1960s, Luke Kelly was playing music in a Dublin pub called The Bailey, which lies just off Grafton Street. As luck would have it, the poet Patrick Kavanagh, now considered one of the greatest poets of the 20th century, was there. "Someone asked him to recite a poem," said Luke, "which he did, and then someone asked me to sing a song, which I did. And then he leaned over to me and said, 'You should sing my song... Raglan Road.' So he gave me permission. I got permission from the man himself." The poem Kavanagh was referring to and which Kelly set to the traditional Irish air, "The Dawning of the Day," was published originally as "Dark-Haired Miriam Ran Away." Many great artists, including Van Morrison, Sinead O'Connor and Mark Knopfler, have covered this haunting song over the years.

Patrick Kavanagh was born in 1904 in County Monaghan and worked as an apprentice shoemaker and also on a small farm. Kavanagh loved nature and was a keen observer of human life— the driving forces behind his poetry. He studied The Arts at Trinity College, Dublin, and eventually settled in Dublin to pursue a literary career. In his late 30s, he fell passionately in love with a young woman called Hilda Moriarty whom he saw walking on Raglan Road in Dublin every day. But she rejected his love. The poem "Dark-Haired Miriam Ran Away" captures the joy and anguish of this relationship.

Luke Kelly was born in Dublin in 1940 and was a renowned singer and musician famous as a founding member of The Dubliners, an Irish folk band.

A Poem, A Song, A Pub

The meeting of Patrick Kavanagh and Luke Kelly became a reference point for the three Irishmen who created the Raglan Road pub, but only after other possibilities had been explored.

"We wanted to call it Lisdoonvarna," says Paul Nolan. "But it turned out to be difficult to pronounce for Americans." Lisdoonvarna is the site of an annual matchmaking festival where plenty of music making, dancing and drinking take place and is immortalized in a song by Christy Moore. The three Irishmen settled on the pub name "Raglan Road" because, "I loved Paddy Kavanagh's poetry, and John loved Luke Kelly and The Dubliners."

The name was different (it was never going to be "Nolan's," "Cooke's'" or "Dundon's"), and it reflected the fact that this Irish pub would be different from patrons' preconceived notions of Irishness and Irish pubs.

The song for which the pub was named is a beautiful and haunting piece of work about unrequited love. "It's sometimes difficult to say precisely what it means to be Irish," Paul says, "but 'On Raglan Road' helps you to talk about Irish identity because it combines poetry, music, grief, longing and belief."

Starters

Life is about memories. Eating something can often take you back to when you first tasted it. Back to picnics during the endless summer days of childhood or to a bowl of something hot and comforting shared by the fire while snow falls outside.

I find that I draw on my childhood memories whenever I create a dish. I love going back to rediscover things and to make a new start from old remembrances.

Soups

There is something very comforting about a steaming hot bowl of soup. It's a quick snack but one that will warm the cockles of your heart every time.

Soups are simple to make but it's important to make them with loving care. Follow the recipes and cook everything sufficiently, using only the very best ingredients and season everything correctly. The majority of soups can be frozen successfully, then thawed and re-heated, making them a convenient route to a heart-warming snack.

SERVES 4-6

French Onion Soup

This is a really nice simple soup to make because it requires so few ingredients. The secret is to get a really good-quality beef stock, as this really enhances the flavour. It's particularly tasty if you make it the day before, then just reheat it slowly. Can you resist digging in for a day? A thicker version of this soup makes the perfect sauce to accompany the perfect steak.

INGREDIENTS

4 large onions, thinly sliced
100g/3½oz/scant ½ cup butter
2-3 sprigs fresh thyme
3 garlic cloves
2 tsp brown sugar
50g/2oz/½ cup, firmly
packed plain flour
150ml/5fl oz/2/3 cup red wine
1 litre/1¾ pint/4 cups
good-quality beef/chicken
stock (heated)
1 sheet puff pastry
1 egg yolk beaten with
2 tsp water, for egg wash
100g/3½oz grated St. Gall
or Gruyère cheese
salt and pepper

METHOD

In a large pot, melt the butter and add in the onions, garlic and thyme sprigs, then sweat off over a medium heat for about 10 minutes or until they have partially softened, turned brown and caramelised. Add in the brown sugar at this stage and allow it to dissolve completely with the onions.

Next add in the plain flour and use it both to coat the onions and dry up any liquid in the pan. Pour in the wine. It will immediately begin to thicken as it reacts with the flour.

Gradually add the stock to the onion mixture. Season with salt and pepper. Stir slowly and then simmer for about 45 minutes, or until the onions are soft and the soup has reduced.

Now let's add a crusty pastry top to the soup. Roll out the pastry on a lightly floured surface. Using the tops of your serving bowls as a template, allow an extra inch around and cut the pastry into discs. Add the soup to the serving bowls. Lightly brush the edge of each bowl with the egg wash and place a pastry disc on the surface. Brush the pastry with egg wash and sprinkle some cheese on top of each pastry disc.

Place the bowls in a preheated oven at 180°C/350°F/Gas Mark 4 for 12 minutes. Serve immediately.

SERVES 4-6

Prawn Bisque

If you fancy a more intense flavour to your bisque, you can blitz the prawn shells, too, in a food processor. But to avoid a grainy texture, you need to really blitz the bejaysus out of the poor shells.

INGREDIENTS

1kg/2lb 4oz prawn shells
1 tbsp butter
1 onion, roughly chopped
2 carrots, trimmed,
roughly chopped
1 celery stalk, trimmed,
roughly chopped
4 sprigs thyme
2 bay leaves
3 sprigs tarragon
¼ tsp cayenne pepper
1 tbsp tomato purée
60ml/2fl oz/generous 3/8 cup
white wine
25ml/1fl oz/1/8 cup brandy
1.2 litres/2 pints/5⅓
cups fish stock, heated
100ml/3½fl oz/scant
½ cup double cream
½ lemon, juice only
50g/1¾ oz/3 generous
tbsp butter
salt and pepper

METHOD

Heat 1 tablespoon butter in a large frying pan until foaming, then add the onion, carrots, celery and herbs and stir well. Fry for 2-3 minutes, or until the vegetables have softened.

Add the prawn shell pieces, cayenne pepper and tomato purée and cook for a further 1-2 minutes.

Pour in the white wine and brandy and remove from the heat. Now here's the ever so slightly scary bit that looks impressive. First, ensure that your extractor fan is turned off. Next, tilt the pan sideways and add a match to the soup, taking care to keep the flames well away from your face, hands and any other objects in the vicinity. Let the flames flare up, then die down and return the pan to the heat. *Phew!*

Add the hot fish stock and bring to the boil, then reduce the heat and simmer the mixture for 30 minutes. Using a slotted spoon, remove the prawn shell pieces and discard them unless you're going to blitz them too (see above). Allow the mixture to cool slightly, then transfer to a food processor and blend to a purée. Finally, pass it through a sieve or fine muslin to obtain a clear stock.

Add the cream and bring to the boil for a minute or so. Remove from the heat. Add the lemon juice and season to taste, with salt and freshly ground black pepper. Finish by adding 50g/1¾ oz/scant 4 tablespoons butter and stirring through the soup. Serve immediately.

Colcannon Soup

I serve this soup with my more-ish cheese straws (see below), which are a fantastic canapé and perfect to kickstart any dinner party. They can be made up to three days in advance and stored in an airtight container at room temperature. Crisp them in a preheated oven at 200°C/400°F/Gas Mark 6 for 2-3 minutes before serving.

INGREDIENTS

4 slices Parma ham
55g/2oz streaky bacon
(rind removed), diced
1 onion, finely chopped
225g/8oz potatoes, diced
1 leek, trimmed and
thinly sliced
150g/5½oz Savoy cabbage,
thick stalks removed
and shredded
700ml/1½ pints/generous
3 cups vegetable stock or
water, heated
150ml/5fl oz/⅔ cup cream
25g/1oz/2 tbsp butter, diced
and at room temperature

Cheese Straws
175g/6oz sheet ready-rolled
puff pastry, thawed if frozen
plain flour, for dusting
55g/2oz cheddar, finely grated
1 egg yolk beaten with 2 tsp
water, for egg wash
salt and pepper

METHOD

Preheat the oven to 180°C/350°F/ Gas Mark 4. To make the cheese straws, place the puff pastry on a lightly floured work surface and sprinkle over the Cheddar in an even layer. Fold in half widthways to completely enclose the cheese layer and roll out again to its original size, using a little extra flour if necessary. Brush all over with the beaten egg and place in the fridge for 15 minutes to rest.

Take the chilled cheese pastry and cut it into 10cm/4 inch lengths, each 1cm/½ inch wide. Twist the ends in opposite directions. Arrange the twisted strips on non-stick baking sheets and sprinkle a little salt over each one. Bake for 10 minutes or until crisp and golden brown, then transfer to a wire rack and leave to cool.

To make the crispy Parma ham shards, use 4 slices of Parma ham and arrange on a baking sheet lined with greaseproof paper. Bake in the oven at 180°C/350°F/Gas Mark 4 for 5 minutes until crispy and then set aside to cool.

Heat a large pan and sauté the bacon over a medium to high heat for a couple minutes. Reduce to a low heat, then add the onion, potatoes, leek and cabbage. Cover with a lid and cook for 10 minutes until well softened but not coloured, stirring occasionally. Pour the warm vegetable stock or water into the cabbage mixture and bring to the boil, then season to taste. Stir in the cream and simmer for a few minutes until the soup has a creamy texture.

Remove the soup from the heat and whisk in the butter. It is important not to re-boil the soup once the butter has been added, or you'll find it will curdle. Ladle the colcannon soup into cappuccino cups or serving bowls, scatter the Parma ham shards on top with an artistic flourish and serve immediately with the cheese straws.

SERVES 4-6

Wild Forest Mushroom Soup

For a real wow factor, serve this soup in brown soda bread containers.

INGREDIENTS

2 tsp olive oil
125g butter/4½oz/generous
½ cup, diced and at room
temperature
150g/5½oz onion,
finely chopped
1 garlic clove, crushed
550g/1lb 4oz forest
mushrooms, such as
chanterelle, oyster or shiitake
mushrooms, chopped
120ml/4fl oz/generous
½ cup white wine
900ml/1½ pints/4 cups
vegetable stock or water
150ml/5fl oz/⅔ cup cream
salt and pepper

To garnish
toasted pine nuts
flat-leaf parsley
forest mushrooms

METHOD

To make the soup, heat a heavy-based pan, then add the olive oil and a knob of the butter. Once the butter is foaming, tip in the onion, garlic and mushrooms and cook slowly for 4-5 minutes until tender but not coloured. Take out and reserve some of the mushroom mixture to garnish.

Add the wine to the pan and allow to evaporate until reduced by half, then season to taste. Add the vegetable stock or water, stirring to combine and bring to the boil. Reduce the heat and simmer for 15-20 minutes until slightly reduced and all the flavours have had the chance to infuse.

Stir the cream into the pan and leave to simmer for another few minutes, then transfer to a food processor or liquidiser and whizz the lot to a purée.

Toast the pine nuts in a hot pan over a medium heat for 3-5 minutes.

To serve, remove the soup from the heat and whisk in the remaining butter.

Season to taste and ladle into brown soda bread containers or warmed serving bowls, then garnish with the toasted pine nuts, torn flat-leaf parsley and mushrooms.

THE STORY OF 'RAGLAN ROAD'

Raglan Road Irish Pub and Restaurant is the first authentic Irish pub in America owned, designed and managed by Irish people. There are many American Irish bars, but none of them is remotely like a traditional Irish pub that you might find in Dublin today.

So how did Raglan Road find its way across the ocean to Orlando, Florida? It is a long story. There is a "road" to Raglan Road that crosses several continents and centuries—a journey involving brewers, publicans, singers, statues, gold rushes, a chef, a poet, yeast, several fishermen and an ex-priest. In short, our story is part of the larger Irish story of misfortune, emigration, hard work, ingenuity and eventual success outside mother Ireland. Come walk the road to Raglan Road with us and stop, now and then, to cook some of Kevin's tasty recipes. Remember, there's a great pub at the end of it. That should be motivation enough, shouldn't it?

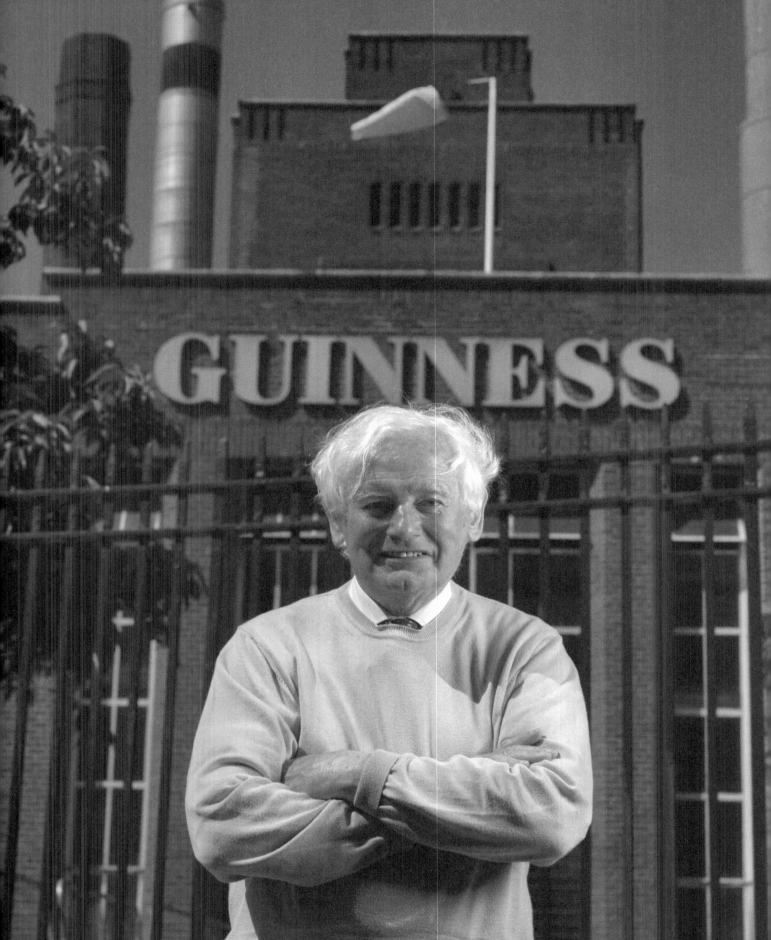

THE ROAD TO RAGLAN ROAD: THE JOURNEY BEGINS

St. James's Gate Brewery, Rialto, Dublin, Ireland.
Frank Nolan: Legend

Our journey begins on August 6, 1950, when a 14-year-old Dublin boy walked through the gates of one of the largest breweries in the world for his very first day of work. The young boy's name was Frank Nolan, and it was his birthday. The brewery, founded in 1759 by Arthur Guinness, was located at St. James's Gate in Dublin. Frank did not know it on his first day working for Guinness, but he was destined to play his part in helping Irish pubs conquer the world over the next few decades.

Frank began work in quality control but managed to get a job in the Guinness laboratory after studying hard at night to earn his qualifications. He then spent seven years in the lab before moving on to the statistics department. But his most significant career move came when he entered the company's marketing division.

Frank created TV advertisements at a time when Guinness ads were redefining how the beverage industry sold its products. He began working with a Dublin advertising company that developed iconic TV ads for Guinness in the 1970s. Ads like "30 Seconds Of Darkness," made when Frank was there, showed a pint of Guinness settling to a classical piano accompaniment and set a new creative standard for beer advertising that influenced the industry for decades. At the same time he was making ads, Frank was taking reports from different regions looking for opportunities and, during this period, research indicated there might be a market for a "lite" version of Guinness.

"At the time, there were Miller Lite and Bud Light in America, so why not Guinness Lite?" he wondered. But this trend, while profitable for lagers, proved to be incompatible with a stout like Guinness. The "lite" drink was heavily marketed by the company with an eye on American sales but panned by the Irish press at its 1979 launch. The negative media coverage killed the new drink among a very conservative drinking fraternity. The beer, cruelly dubbed "the HMS Titanic of stout products" by the Irish Times, was retired soon after. The setback didn't hurt Frank's career, which soon took another direction.

Frank became involved in Guinness's studies of an intriguing phenomenon that kept cropping up in sales reports—the outstanding performance of the Irish pub in foreign lands.

"They found that disproportionate sales were made in Irish pubs abroad and wanted to find a formula that might work for them," he explains.

Guinness took a long, hard look at the success of Irish pubs that had opened outside of Ireland and decided that these pubs had four crucial factors in common that led to success: Irish owners or managers; good music and entertainment; great food; and, most important, they ran their businesses exactly as pubs would be run in Ireland to create a friendly, vibrant atmosphere. These four factors became the basis for the best Irish pubs that would spring up across the world over the next three decades.

The Great Irish Pub Invasion

Our journey moves from Dublin to Germany soon after Guinness identified 100 existing pubs outside of Ireland that fit their formula of what constituted the successful Irish pub abroad. Many of the pubs were in Germany because, as Frank explains, "The Germans just seem to have a good affinity with Ireland." They had been opened by Irish ex-pats who popped up on the Guinness marketing radar because of their unusually high sales of draught Guinness. Guinness pondered the idea of copying their formula for success in order to boost sales by opening more Irish pubs around Europe.

Though Frank left Guinness in 1984 after 34 years at the company, he returned soon after to help develop a new network of Irish pubs across Europe. The idea was to recruit bar staff and pub managers in Ireland by offering them ownership.

This would have been a great opportunity at any time, but it was especially appealing given the poor state of the Irish economy in the 1980s. Guinness also appreciated that Irish people were willing to emigrate for work and show what they could achieve outside of Ireland.

Guinness opened pubs in clusters in the same European city so that if you visited one Irish pub in, say, Hamburg there would be another one 200 yards down the road. They went to great lengths to get the pubs right, even finding the bands needed to give the German pubs an authentic Irish atmosphere.

"Guinness found the bands, then sent them out for a month or two on a small tour of six to eight Irish pubs," Frank said. "The bands made good money, enjoyed themselves and recruited dancers from Ireland, so it was the whole package."

The same approach worked in France, where Guinness tweaked the concept to be a bit more upmarket.

"We picked locations in better-class areas of French cities—a good move because the French wouldn't travel to less savory areas of their cities to drink Guinness." The pubs developed in Paris succeeded, even though France had never before been a good market for draught Guinness.

Frank, now retired, is understandably proud of what his son, Paul, has achieved at Raglan Road by creating what he calls "the best Irish pub in the world" some 60 years after he first walked through the gates of Guinness in Dublin.

Frank helped create one of the most successful global food-and-beverage concepts of the 20th and 21st centuries—the Irish pub. But stimulus for the next phase of growth came from a very unlikely quarter.

In 1986, Ireland appointed Jack Charlton—member of England's World Cup winning team in 1966—to be the country's national soccer manager, and the Irish soccer team began the most successful streak in its history. What does soccer have to do with Irish pubs? Why did more than 100 Irish pubs open in Italy in 1991? The next stop on the road to Raglan Road takes us on a tour of Europe.

1988 AND ALL THAT...

Vasil Levsky Stadium, Sofia, Bulgaria.
Gary Mackay: Soccer Player

The next leg of our journey takes us to Sofia in Bulgaria on the night of November 11, 1987. At the Vasil Levsky National Stadium, the Bulgarian soccer team was playing a Euro '88 qualifying game against Scotland on a chilly winter's evening when, with three minutes left to play, Gary Mackay cut in from the right, and his shot ended up in the bottom corner of the Bulgarian net. Scotland won the match 1-0, but the victory was not enough for the team to qualify. It did, however, mean that Ireland qualified for a major soccer tournament for the first time ever—a pretty significant event for the whole of Ireland. There were wild celebrations.

Irish soccer fans had loyally followed their team during the qualifiers hoping for victories in Bulgaria, Belgium and Luxembourg, as well as Scotland, and were rewarded with success. The new national team manager, Jack Charlton, had turned the fortunes of the Irish soccer team around with a mixture of simple tactics and a greater belief. Everywhere the fans went, they found the local Irish pubs and settled in to enjoy themselves. The locals joined in and saw, first hand, the charm of Irish hospitality. They decided they liked it. Guinness noticed that on the dates of soccer matches Irish pubs in the European cities hosting the matches generated more revenue than 100 of their other accounts put together. At a time when the game was plagued by hooliganism and traveling supporters were often greeted with suspicion and a heavy police presence, Irish fans earned a reputation for knowing how to enjoy themselves in a peaceful manner and getting on extremely well with their local hosts.

Ireland's supporters next went to the Euro '88 Finals in Germany and were rewarded by watching their team beat rivals England 1-0 in Stuttgart and draw 1-1 with Russia in Hannover before losing 1-0 to Holland in Gelsenkirchen. The soccer team then qualified for the "Italia '90" World Cup, where they went as far as the quarter finals before being beaten 1-0 by hosts Italy in Rome.

By the end of the following year, more than 100 Irish pubs had opened in Italy, as the Italians decided they wanted to keep the party atmosphere generated by Irish fans going permanently. During the European Irish pub influx, a new business called the Irish Pub Company was appointed by Guinness to be their sole Irish pub concept designer.

The Irish Pub Company evolved the four factors of successful Irish pubs that Guinness had originally discovered into Five Fundamentals—good Irish food, Irish staff, a mix of Irish drinks, great entertainment and authentic Irish pub design. Established in 1991, the Irish Pub Company researched the origins, history and styles of pubs in great depth, then designed, manufactured and installed them across the world, creating successful businesses in very different cultures.

For further insight into the expansion of Irish pubs worldwide, we need to meet a man who helped fit them out. The road to Raglan Road takes us next to a tense Moscow in August of 1991, where tanks are about to roll onto the streets. Just as one empire has begun to crumble, another one is spreading eastward.

SERVES 4-6

Creamy Potato & Lime Soup

This is a delicious soup. It has a lovely consistency and is nice and warming on those cold winter days. It's the sort of soup you'll end up putting in a flask and bringing out with you to school, to work or anywhere you go.

INGREDIENTS

5-6 large potatoes
55g/2oz/¼ cup butter
1 large onion,
chopped roughly
3 garlic cloves, crushed
1 large leek, chopped
2 bay leaves
about 1.2 litres/2 pints/
5⅓ cups well-flavoured chicken
stock
150ml/5fl oz/⅔ cup cream
salt and pepper
zest and juice of 1 lime

METHOD

Begin by peeling the potatoes for the soup and chop them into large chunks. Melt the butter in a large saucepan and add in the chopped onion, garlic and leeks.

Sweat the vegetables off for approximately 6-8 minutes over a gentle heat until they are softened down. Add in the bay leaves and the chopped potatoes at this time – it's their turn to sweat for a moment or two. Season the mixture lightly at this stage.

Now pour in the warm chicken stock and the cream and allow the entire mixture to come to the boil. I normally add only about two-thirds of the required amount of stock at this stage and add the remainder later on.

It is difficult with this soup to exactly quantify the amount of stock required because the size of the potatoes varies greatly.

Once the soup comes to the boil, boil it for about 2-3 minutes and then reduce to a gentle heat. Simmer for an additional 10-15 minutes until the potatoes have softened. Remove the bay leaves.

Blitz the soup with a hand blender, adding additional stock if you like your soup thin. Correct the seasoning of the soup and reheat it gently.

Squeeze the lime juice over the soup and sprinkle with lime zest. Serve immediately.

Kevin's tip
You can crumble some creamy blue cheese on top of the soup as a garnish to offer a contrast with the sharpness of the lime.

SERVES 4-6

Roasted Butternut Squash Soup

This is a delicious soup, which you can prepare well in advance of a meal. I suggest you serve this soup in a china cup at a dinner party, as sometimes a large bowl can be too filling. But, however you present it, this soup will definitely be the toast of the party.

INGREDIENTS

2 carrots
1 leek
2 celery stalks
1 large butternut squash
½ medium onion
3 garlic cloves
55g/2oz/¼ cup butter
pinch of crushed chilli flakes
175ml/6fl oz/¾ cup cream
1.2 litres/2 pints/5⅓ cups chicken/vegetable stock
salt and pepper

METHOD

Begin by peeling and chopping all of the vegetables into uniform-sized pieces. Select a large saucepan and slowly melt the butter. Add in all of the vegetables, mix thoroughly and continue to roast them for 6-8 minutes. Keep stirring the vegetables to prevent them from sticking to the saucepan. Season lightly at this stage, then add the chilli flakes.

Next you need to add in the cream and two-thirds of the stock. Bring this mixture to the boil and then reduce the heat to a constant simmer.

Simmer for the next 15-20 minutes or until all of the vegetables have softened.

Blitz the soup until smooth, using your blitzing device of choice – liquidizer, food processor or hand blender – and adjusting the consistency with the remaining stock as required.

Taste the soup and season accordingly. Feeling daring? Why not add in extra chilli flakes?

Kevin's tip
This soup is suitable for freezing. Keep it for up to 1 month in the freezer.

THE COLOUR DOESN'T MATCH THE MYTHS

Throughout history, people have portrayed the Irish as having red hair, pale skin and a sprinkling of freckles. But the truth is that only about 9 percent of Irish people are redheads and only 5 percent are really true reds. The rest might be called auburn, coppery or russet-haired. Anything, in fact, except the dreaded "R" word. The reality is that brown is the most common Irish hair colour with about half of the Irish having dark brown locks.

If any nationality deserves a reputation for red-headedness, it has to be the Scots and, even then, only 13 percent of Scottish are red on top. So how did the Irish reputation for red locks evolve? Red hair is said to have originated in Europe about 40,000 years ago by genetic mutation, but it still remains rare among the world population. It's probably just the distinctiveness of the hair colour that earned the Irish this reputation as they spread all across the world. It was something people remembered.

Disadvantages of fiery curls

Truth is, if your hair is red, others often assume the worst about your character. Fiery, impulsive, reckless—redheads have a hard time overturning the negative stereotypes. In the Middle Ages, redheads were accused of being in league with the devil and were persecuted. Today, scientists reckon that reds need 20 percent more anaesthetic because they have a lower pain threshold. It turns out that the gene that controls the red-hair pigment also stimulates a brain receptor linked to pain sensitivity.

Despite the disadvantages, some redheads have made names for themselves over the years including our very own James Joyce, as well as Cleopatra and Malcolm X, who inherited his red hair colour from his Scottish maternal grandfather. And then there are the infamous. Oliver Cromwell and Lizzie Borden were also known for their red tresses.

"Being Irish, he had an abiding sense of tragedy, which sustained him through temporary periods of joy." WB Yeats (Irish poet)

SERVES 4-6

Tomato & Gin Soup

This is one of my favourite 'empty larder' recipes that requires little preparation and is quick to cook. Simple.

INGREDIENTS

2 tbsp olive oil
1 small onion, finely chopped
2 garlic cloves, finely chopped
1kg/2lb 4oz ripe plum
tomatoes, halved
60ml/2fl oz/generous
⅜ cup gin
700ml/1¼ pints/3 cups
vegetable stock or water
1 pinch light muscovado
sugar, optional
225ml/8fl oz/1 cup cream
salt and pepper
1 tbsp herb oil, to garnish

METHOD

Heat the olive oil in a pan over a medium-high heat. Add the onion and garlic and sauté for a few minutes until golden. Add the tomatoes and continue to sauté for another 5 minutes or so until well heated through and just beginning to break down. Season with salt and pepper.

Pour the gin into the pan and allow to reduce by half, stirring occasionally. Stir in the vegetable stock or water and allow to reduce by half again.

Blitz with a hand blender to a smooth purée. Season to taste and add the sugar if you think the soup needs it.

To serve, add the cream to the soup and allow to warm through. Season to taste and ladle into warmed serving bowls. Garnish each bowl with a drizzle of herb oil.

SERVES 6

Hearty Irish Broth & Barley

This is the sort of soup that pleads to be eaten when you are feeling tired and jaded. Serve it with some warm crusty bread slathered with butter – delicious! I like to make it in the autumn when plum tomatoes are at their best and in ample supply.

INGREDIENTS

200g/7oz/1 cup pearl barley
2 tbsp olive oil
1 onion, chopped
½ green cabbage, thick stalks
removed and shredded
1 leek, thinly sliced
2 carrots, thinly diced
8 ripe plum tomatoes, diced
120ml/4fl oz/generous
½ cup dry white wine
1 litre/1¾ pints/scant
4½ cups kitchen garden
vegetable stock or water
salt and pepper
fresh flat-leaf parsley
sprigs, to garnish

METHOD

Place the pearl barley in a bowl and pour in cold water ensuring all the barley is covered. Leave it to soak for 2-5 hours.

Heat the olive oil in a large pan and add the onion, cabbage, leek and carrots, stirring to combine. Cover with a lid and sweat over a medium heat for about 5 minutes until softened but not coloured.

Add the tomatoes to the pan, season to taste and allow to cook for a couple of minutes.

Pour in the wine and allow to reduce by half, then add the stock or water and bring to the boil. Season to taste. Reduce the heat and leave to simmer for 10 minutes until all of the vegetables are completely tender and the liquid has slightly reduced and thickened. Add the soaked pearl barley and simmer for a further 20 minutes until the barley has softened.

To serve, ladle the soup into warmed serving bowls. Garnish with freshly chopped herbs.

Paul is the one on the right

CAN YOU BUILD A PUB FOR ME?

Moscow Airport, Moscow, Russia.
Paul Hamilton: Irish Pub Specialist 'Extraordinaire'

Our journey continues in Russia where, on August 19, 1991, tanks from two armoured divisions of the Soviet army rumbled into Moscow accompanied by paratroopers. A military coup against President Mikhail Gorbachev had begun. At the same time that hardliners in the KGB, alarmed by the imminent breakup of the Soviet Union, had decided to take control by force, the first pints of draught Guinness were being pulled at an Irish pub in Moscow airport. The coup failed, but Irish pubs became a permanent feature in Russia and ex-Soviet Union countries as the empire finally collapsed. One of the people responsible for their enduring success was the person who fitted them out, Sligo man, Paul Hamilton.

Paul was born in Sligo Town, County Sligo, and grew up on the west coast of Ireland. His father was from Dromahair, County Leitrim, and his mother hailed from Easkey, County Sligo. His grandfather had a Sligo pub called Hamilton's in the 1930s but eventually, the pub passed out of the family. A love of Irish pubs must have been passed down to Paul in the genes, however, even if it took time to make itself known.

"I'm from a generation that grew up in Ireland but never expected to work there," Paul explains.

He left the country, as did many thousands of others, in the 1970s and spent time working as an engineer in London, then Saudi Arabia, before returning and marrying in the 1980s. "It was still pretty grim in Ireland in the 1980s, and I soon left again," he says. Paul ran a company called MDA Shop Fitting that fitted and opened the first Irish pubs and shops in Russia. He was working in the heart of the Soviet Union just as it was falling apart. If times were grim in Ireland, they were very dark, indeed, in the old Soviet empire.

"I remember doing a shop front in Tblisi," Paul recalls, "and a crowd formed trying to figure out how the guys were working without cables because the Georgians had never seen battery-operated drills before."

Paul fitted out the Arbat Irish House pub in a downtown Moscow shopping area and the first Irish pub at Moscow Airport. With a pint's costing $2.50 in the early 1990s and the average Russian monthly wage at just $10, the customers were mainly foreigners and Muscovites living off dubious earnings.

Paul remembers seeing elderly ladies brushing snow off the pavements of Moscow at 6 a.m. as he headed to work. They had been born around the time the Soviet Union was created in 1922. They had survived Stalin's purges in the 1930s and the invasion by the Nazis during the Second World War, enduring unimaginable hardships for decades.

"These were women who believed in communism with the same reverence that my parents believed in the Catholic Church back home in Ireland." He could see that they had given their lives to communism, and here it was crumbling around them, day by day, until it collapsed utterly.

"I remember seeing a crowd trying to tear down a statue of Stalin in Tblisi in Georgia, which is not far from where he was born in Gori. They tore it all down except for a leg. The next day when I went past, the leg was gone too."

Paul worked for the Irish Pub Company, attending Guinness investor road shows where people would come up to him and say, "can you build a pub for me?"

"I was probably directly involved in around 500 of them," he says. Paul spent the 1990s traveling the world and opening Irish pubs on six-week-long trips to up to 20 cities, flying Dublin-London-Singapore-Perth-Sydney-Melbourne-Cairns-Tokyo-Osaka-Bejing-Shanghai. "My wife jokes that the reason we've been married for 30 years is because I've been away for most of them."

The spread of Irish pubs across the world took him to some remote places. He remembers doing two pubs in Novosibirsk, Russia's third-largest city in central Siberia, where winter temperatures can dip to minus 50 degrees centigrade. "That's the coldest place I've ever been."

In Perth, Western Australia, he fitted out a pub in Burswood Entertainment Complex. The pub was called Paddy Hannan's after the Irishman from County Clare who, in 1893, discovered one of the largest gold seams in the world in Kalgoorlie, western Australia, and started a gold rush. In its first year, Paddy Hannan's had a larger turnover than the rest of the complex's food and beverage outlets put together.

In 1996, he moved on to Mainland China and opened O'Malley's in Shanghai for Rob Young, an investor from New Zealand. But there was one big problem. Young wanted an Irish husband-and-wife team to run the pub, so Paul suggested placing an ad in Ireland's Sunday Independent. In the ad, Young made the mistake of mentioning Guinness. The company was not happy that its name was associated with the venture.

"When they saw it, they said there was no way they were supplying draught Guinness to Mainland China, even though they already had it 750 miles away in Hong Kong." Paul just could not understand Guinness's hesitance until he discovered the company was concerned that its steel draught beer kegs, costing 30 euros each, would not be returned when empty. Once Young personally guaranteed the kegs' return, Guinness backed the project and the pub became one of the biggest success stories of 1996.

The Irish Pub Company insisted upon authentic Irish names for all the new pubs, and Paul often suggested "Hamilton's" after his grandfather's pub back in Sligo. But only one pub—based in the town of Hamilton, New Zealand—ever adopted the name. So when a Russian investor named Konstantine asked Paul if he could name his pub "Hamilton's," he was flattered. The pub was in Belgorod, Russia, 11 hours south of Moscow by train and close to Kursk, where the biggest tank battle of World War II took place.

Konstantine obsessed over every detail to get his pub authentically Irish. He flew Paul and his wife down to Belgorod in 2007, and they were met at the airport with bunches of flowers. When Paul and his wife arrived at the pub, they discovered that Konstantine had taken a picture of Paul and commissioned an Ukranian artist to create a beautiful copper sculpture of his face, which he proudly presented to Paul.

"My wife did not stop laughing for three days," he recalls, noting that Hamilton's of Belgorod has become one of his favourite Irish pubs in the world.

Paul assisted at the opening of Raglan Road Irish Pub & Restaurant, traveling to Florida to get an understanding of the operational requirements. The concept design that evolved was very much influenced by owners Paul Nolan and John Cooke. The finished project, says Paul Hamilton, "is the result of the collective experience of three people who have been involved in pubs all over the world." The work was an Irish-American co-production in which Paul controlled the design and supply of the fit-out elements from Dublin, but worked with a local architect and building contractors for the installation of those elements.

"Helping to open Irish pubs was one of those jobs that, if I'd been younger, I would have totally lost the run of myself," he admits. He says he left the job eventually because it had become a "lifestyle. I said to myself 'I can't spend the rest of my life doing this.' I do miss it though," he adds wistfully.

We've covered plenty of ground on the journey to Raglan Road, but there is one question that we have not yet addressed. What precisely is an Irish pub? To find out, we'll time travel back nearly four centuries to Ireland at the time of the Viking invasions.

Roast Carrot & Garlic Soup

This is a really nice, highly flavoured soup that is great to enjoy on cold winter days. It also freezes quite well, so it's a great recipe to have on standby in the freezer.

INGREDIENTS

5 carrots, cut into batons
1 bulb of garlic, broken
into cloves and peeled
1 tbsp olive oil
55g/2oz/¼ cup butter
½ medium onion,
thinly sliced
1 leek, finely sliced
1 small celery stalk,
finely chopped
75ml/3fl oz/⅓ cup cream
1.2 litres/2 pints/5⅓ cups
chicken/vegetable stock
salt and pepper
4 tsp crème fraiche,
to garnish

METHOD

Preheat the oven to 180°C/350°F/ Gas Mark 4. Place the carrot batons and garlic on a baking tray and drizzle them with olive oil. Place in the preheated oven for 30-40 minutes until softened and roasted.

Select a large saucepan and slowly melt the butter. Add the onions, leek and celery and sauté gently. Add the roasted carrot and vegetables. Add in the cream and two-thirds of the stock. Why only two-thirds? Because I find it's best to add only some of the stock, as it allows you to adjust or correct the consistency more accurately before serving.

Bring this mixture to the boil, then reduce the heat to a constant simmer. Simmer for 10-15 minutes or until all of the vegetables have softened.

Pour the soup mixture into a food processor and blitz the living daylights out of the soup until smooth, adjusting the consistency with the remaining stock as required. Taste the soup and season accordingly.

Garnish the soup with a little crème fraiche. You can spice things up with a few chilli flakes if the mood takes you.

Kevin's tip
Try substituting the carrot and garlic for pumpkin and butternut squash, or sweet potatoes and parsnips, or try an extended mixture of vegetables including carrots, leeks, celery and onion.

Leek & Potato Soup

This thick and creamy soup is both hearty enough to satisfy your appetite and comforting enough to leave you feeling good.

INGREDIENTS

25g/1oz/2 tbsp butter
4-5 large leeks, cleaned
 and finely sliced
1 medium onion, finely sliced
3 potatoes, peeled and diced
850ml/1½ pints/3¾ cups
stock or water, warmed
275ml/10fl oz/1¼ cups cream
salt and pepper

To serve
1 tbsp crème fraiche or
double cream
1 tsp fresh oregano or parsley

METHOD

In a large pan gently melt the butter, then add the leeks, onions and potatoes, stirring them all round with a wooden spoon so they get a lovely coating of butter. Season with salt and pepper, then cover and let the vegetables sweat over a very low heat for about 5 minutes.

After that, add the stock or water and bring to simmering point. Cover and let the soup simmer very gently for a further 20 minutes, or until the vegetables are softened.

Using a hand blender, blitz the soup and then pass it through a fine sieve.

Return the soup to the saucepan and reheat gently, tasting to check the seasoning. Add a fancy swirl of cream or crème fraîche before serving and sprinkle with fresh oregano or parsley.

A VERY PUBLIC HOUSE

The Brazen Head Pub, Dublin, Ireland.
Dubliners: Pub Goers

It is time for a detour in our journey back to the time of the Viking conquest of Ireland. In 1198, the Brazen Head Pub opened in Dublin and is still open for business today, making it the city's oldest pub. History doesn't record whether the first customers were Vikings or Celts, but the pub is evidence of a tradition of brewing that stretches back even farther in time. Medieval monks in monasteries all over Ireland were renowned for brewing at a time when water purity was suspect and it was often safer to drink ale than risk the local H2O. Beer has been brewed ever since man first discovered the magic of fermentation. Indeed, some archaeologists believe that the "fulacht fiadh"—the horseshoe-shaped, grass-covered mounds found across Ireland—were used as Bronze Age breweries more than 2,500 years ago.

Pubs, also known as public houses, began as private homes that were licensed to sell beer and spirits by the families that ran them and lived there. Families commonly began by opening up a downstairs room—typically the dining room—as a "social room" and installing a bar. When they finished business for the day, they locked up and retired to sleep "above the shop." If business was really good, they opened the kitchen, too, and even converted bedrooms upstairs for public use. It was common to use the family name as the pub name; hence, pub names like Whelan's, Doherty's or Mahon's.

The pub soon became the social heart of Irish towns and villages. Pubs didn't just sell alcohol, but diversified with necessities like fruit, vegetables, meat and bread. Some sold more unusual goods like bicycles and fishing tackle. Pubs even doubled as undertakers. In 1846, Ireland's Coroner's Act decreed that a dead body could be directed to a public house, and the owner was obliged to house the corpse, so some enterprising owners began undertaking businesses as a profitable sideline.

Pubs often incorporated a "bar" and a "snug"—two different rooms separated by timber or glass screens which came right up to the serving area. Men drank in the bar. Women sipped in the snug. The snug evolved into the lounge, over time, and was marginally more luxurious than the basic bar, with slightly pricier drinks.

Traditional music has been long associated with Irish pubs, with some pubs earning great reputations for their community-based entertainment. Locals would sing or bring their own instruments, but the main component has always been warmth and hospitality. The fact that a family's livelihood depended on knowing everyone's name and having the right drink ready when a customer walked through the door was critical in establishing a tradition of good service.

The welcoming Irish pub interiors began with a lick of paint and soon became adorned with brightly coloured signs or prints of advertisements. As publicans and shopkeepers increased the practice of prominently displaying the ads, the phenomenon of Irish pub bric-a-brac evolved.

Ornaments and oddments that included many Guinness signs and advertisements earned spots around the pub as decoration. The next stop on the road to Raglan Road introduces us to the king of bric-a-brac. In the early 1980s, just as he is forced to close his own pub near Dundalk in Ireland, the bric-a-brac king is about to discover his unique role in the unstoppable growth of the Irish pub.

Salads

Whether the salad will be a side dish or a nutritious entrée, it doesn't have to be restricted to a scattering of green leaves and sliced tomatoes. Be creative. Unleash your lettuce. Sure, it's great to master a classic like a Caesar Salad, but salads can be formed from an infinite number of taste partnerships using combinations like the creaminess of Irish cashel blue cheese with the sweetness of caramelized pecans, the peppery sweetness of basil with ripe plum tomatoes or the sweetness of cannellini, kidney and garbanzo beans with the sharpness of apple cider vinegar.

And salads don't have to be eaten cold. My Grilled Mediterranean Salad combines fresh grilled vegetables with balsamic vinegar. Remember, just because salads are a healthful choice doesn't mean

Caesar Salad

Many of us like to order Caesar salad when we eat out, but back home we never seem to know how to go about the preparation of this very simple dish. This is my recipe for this firm favourite with a bit of a Dundon difference thrown in. Hail Caesar!

INGREDIENTS

1 garlic clove, chopped
1 tsp capers
3 anchovies, chopped
(use more or fewer
depending on your taste)
200g/7oz Parmesan
cheese, grated plus extra
shavings to garnish
40–50ml/1½–2fl oz/about 3 tbsp
Worcestershire sauce
½ tbsp cracked black pepper
2 egg yolks
2 tbsp lemon juice
1 tsp Dijon mustard
200ml/7fl oz/generous
¾ cup sunflower oil
1 tsp water
1 medium ciabatta loaf
or 4 thick slices crusty
white bread
salt
2 tbsp olive oil
8 thin slices of dried prosciutto
1 large cos or romaine
lettuce, leaves separated
8 cherry tomatoes, halved

METHOD

Combine the sliced garlic, capers, anchovies, grated Parmesan cheese, Worcestershire sauce and cracked pepper in a large bowl. Mix with a handheld blender or food processor until it turns into a smooth purée.

In a second bowl, prepare a mayonnaise by combining the egg yolks, lemon juice and the Dijon mustard and whisk until smooth. Drizzle in the sunflower oil in a slow and steady stream while whisking. You can use a food processor or blender until it forms a thick consistency.

Fold in the puréed ingredients. Season to taste, and add 1 teaspoon water to loosen up the mixture a little.

Preheat the oven to 200°C/400°F/ Gas Mark 6. Tear the bread into big, ragged croutons or, if you prefer a more precise approach, cut with a bread knife into cubes. Spread over a large baking sheet or tray and sprinkle over 2 tablespoons of olive oil. Rub the oil into the bread and season. Bake for 8-10 minutes, turning the croutons a few times during cooking so they are evenly browned.

Prepare the prosciutto by placing it on a flat tray, then bake in the oven for 8–10 minutes until crispy. Remove from the oven, and set aside to cool.

When all the ingredients are ready, toss the salad leaves with the Caesar dressing, the croutons, cherry tomatoes and dried bacon in a large bowl. Serve with some extra Parmesan shavings.

SERVES 4

Cashel Blue Cheese Salad

Cashel Blue cheese is Ireland's first farmhouse blue cheese. It's very versatile and has many culinary uses because it has a slightly creamier consistency and lower salt content than most other blue cheeses.

INGREDIENTS

100g/3½oz prosciutto slices
100g/3½oz/½ cup
superfine sugar
25g/1oz/scant ¼ cup pecans
500g/1lb 2oz green/red oak
lettuce, cleaned and washed
1 bunch watercress,
cleaned and washed
12 cherry tomatoes, halved
100g/3½oz crumbled
Cashel Blue cheese

Vinaigrette
200g/7oz raspberries, fresh
1 lemon juice
1 tbsp honey
100ml/3½fl oz/scant
½ cup olive oil
salt and pepper

METHOD

First prepare the raspberry vinaigrette by combining 100g/3½oz the fresh raspberries with the lemon juice. Use a hand blender and blitz until smooth. Pass through a fine sieve to remove any small seeds.

In a second bowl, pour in the puréed raspberry, then add the honey, olive oil, and seasoning. Whisk to obtain a silky vinaigrette and store until needed. Should the vinaigrette split, whisk gently to recombine it before serving.

Preheat the oven to 200°C/400°F/ Gas Mark 6. Place the prosciutto on a baking sheet and place in the oven for 5–8 minutes until crispy. Remove from the oven, and set aside to cool.

Meanwhile, to caramelise the pecan nuts, place the sugar into a heavy based pan and allow to dissolve over a low heat. When the sugar has completely dissolved, continue to heat until the sugar has turned a rich brown colour, then add the pecan nuts and remove the pan from the heat. Using a spoon, remove the pecans from the pan and place on greaseproof paper and allow to cool.

In a bowl combine the red and green oak leaves, watercress, the remaining raspberries, caramelised pecans, prosciutto, tomatoes, Cashel Blue cheese, vinaigrette and salt, lightly toss being careful not to crush the raspberries. Serve immediately.

FROM WHENCE CAME ALL THIS STUFF?

The Smugglers' Inn, James's Quay, Ireland.
Chas Mclaughlin: The Bric-a-brac King

One day in the early 1980s, Chas McLoughlin found himself standing in the Smugglers' Inn pub in James's Quay, County Louth, removing beautiful old enamel signs from the walls. The Smugglers' Inn was Chas's pub. He had found the signs when touring Ireland on a buying trip with his brother and had displayed them lovingly around the pub. But this day, he was forced to hand over the failed pub and planned to sell all the signs. It looked as if Chas's pub business venture had come to a close but, in fact, it was only just beginning. He would discover soon enough that the bric-a-brac displayed on his pub walls was incredibly popular with buyers, including the partners who created Raglan Road.

Originally from Derry in Northern Ireland, Chas was a teenager in the late 1960s and early '70s during The Troubles—when there was an oppressive British presence on the streets. He had what he describes as a "typical Northern Irish teenage boyhood," but he didn't neglect his studies. He attended St. Columb's College, Derry's oldest and largest Catholic grammar school—an institution that turned out two Nobel laureates, Seamus Heaney and John Hume.

Chas's move into the pub business happened years later when he saw the Smugglers' Inn and thought it might make a good investment. Then came that buying trip when he searched Ireland high and low for just the right bric-a-brac. He started with the things he loves most, "all the old enamel signs, especially in blue and yellow, and a few nice pub mirrors." After giving up his own pub, Chas continued collecting and posted ads in the Irish Independent to sell his treasures. One of his earliest and best customers was Danny Fitzpatrick, owner of Fitzpatrick's, Chas's local pub. When Danny's pub won the "Black & White Pub of the Year" award in 2001, everyone asked him where he got his bric-a-brac. All signs pointed to Chas.

Today, Chas has a warehouse full of just about every object relating to Irish life and drinking you can imagine. Last year, he got a phone call to clear 35,000 original Guinness bottles, a full 40-foot container full of them. He also picked up 800 original whiskey crates from O'Connor's bottling company in County Cork and cleared 500 stoneware jars from Quinn's whiskey bonders in Limerick. Where does all this stuff end up? It turns out that many customers love the authentic flavour that Irish bric-a-brac lends their pubs, and their tastes can be quite eclectic.

Chas has had requests to find materials for pubs with a mining theme in Philadelphia, Pa., and to help decorate a pub with a clothes-shop theme that involved sourcing old-fashioned mannequins. He has even given a hotel bar in Macroom, County Cork, a toy-soldier theme because Macroom has the only remaining factory in Ireland where they still make lead soldiers. Chas combines with ease the skills of a social historian, antiques expert and market trader.

Only once did he feel he went over the top with a pub theme. The request: to supply items for a pub named after Countess Markievicz, the revolutionary Irish nationalist who took part in the 1916 Easter Rising. "I had pictures of the Countess, the bombing of the four courts and some 16lb brass shells," says Chas. "I had a copy of Pearse's surrender letter and some petrol bombs in 12 cabinets. It might have touched a nerve!" The owner was happy, but an angry letter sent to the Donegal Democrat complained that the pub had been named after a "murderess."

The business of decorating Irish pubs draws two very distinct types of customers. "One customer will want an NCR cash register, a particular type of bell and a picture of Nelson's Column. The other will say 'I'm doing an Irish pub—what have you got?'" Publican Martin McCaffrey has ordered plenty of bric-a-brac for his Hole in the Wall pub in Dublin. At Nancy Hand's pub in Parkgate Street, Dublin, Chas supplied ceilings, paneling and tiles salvaged from old Victorian houses. Pub designers come to Chas for fixtures and fittings for traditional-looking Irish pubs in Ireland and around the world. That was how Chas came to the attention of the Irish Pub Company.

He was able to help the Company with one of its Five Fundamentals – authentic Irish design – and his first challenge was Nine Fine Irishmen in Las Vegas. The Company wanted Nine Fine Irishmen to evoke an authentic pre-1900 period. The result was achieved using taxidermy, original rifles and muskets, a range of blacksmith's tools and anvils, old traps and kitchen pots. His work on Nine Fine Irishmen brought Chas into contact with the future owners of Raglan Road. Not only did the Irish owners of Raglan Road buy original Victorian items from Chas, they also asked him to spend a week in Orlando decorating the pub with bric-a-brac.

The cabinet displays in Raglan Road's Music Room include some century-old items; among them, a period phonograph. Chas also supplied a Seltzer, a Hohner accordion, a fiddle and a variety of music manuscripts that pre-date the Second World War. And he sourced items once sold in Irish pubs that doubled as grocery stores such as teapots, tea caddies, and a ceramic hot water bottle at the pub's Paddy's Bar.

Is there any spot in the world where Chas hasn't supplied bric-a-brac? Chas thinks a moment, narrows his eyes and then says, "I don't think I've done Antarctica—yet."

SERVES 4

Heirloom Tomato Salad

*The consommé that accompanies this salad is more than just a clear soup,
it's bursting with freshness and flavour.*

INGREDIENTS

Tomato consommé
8 ripe plum tomatoes
1 small onion
1 garlic clove
200g/7oz basil
seasoning
pinch of superfine sugar

Tomatoes salad
12 cherry plum tomatoes
1 tbsp white balsamic vinegar
2 tbsp extra virgin olive oil
salt and pepper
1 shallot, finely sliced
200g/7oz baby salad leaves,
to line the tuilles

Cheese tuille
100g/3½oz/1 cup cheddar
cheese, grated
about ½ tsp cracked
black pepper

METHOD

Tomato consommé
Place all the ingredients in a
food processor and blitz until
you achieve a smooth tomato
purée. Pour the purée over a
bowl lined with muslin, and
press gently to extract the clear
juice. Repeat this step by pouring
the clear consommé over a fresh
clean muslin-lined bowl, then
correct the seasoning and store
in the fridge until needed.

Tomatoes salad
Halve the tomatoes, then drizzle
with white balsamic vinegar and
virgin olive oil. Toss carefully,
then season with a pinch of
salt and freshly ground black
pepper. Add the sliced shallots
and, using your hands, gently
combine all the ingredients.

Cheese tuille
Heat a non-stick frying pan until
searing hot. Sprinkle a quarter of
the grated cheddar cheese into

the centre of the pan in a circle
about 10cm/4 inches in diameter.
Add a good sprinkling of pepper
and cook for 2-3 minutes until
the fat starts to separate from
the cheese and bubble. Remove
from the heat and leave to cool
for 1 minute.

Using a spatula, remove the
melted cheese disc from the pan.
Shape the cheese basket around
the end of a straight-sided tall
glass and hold for 30 seconds
to 1 minute until set. Transfer
to a wire rack and allow to cool
completely. Repeat with the
remaining ingredients until you
have four cheese baskets in total.

Serve the tomato salad
immediately with some baby
green salad leaves, a serving
of tomato consommé and a
cheese tuille.

SERVES 4

Mixed Bean Salad

This is a quick and easy salad that can be prepared up to 24 hours in advance to allow the flavours to develop. You can alter the recipe to suit whatever beans you have and add some spicy additions if you wish!

INGREDIENTS

400g/14oz canned cannellini beans, rinsed and drained
400g/14oz canned kidney beans, rinsed and drained
200g/7oz canned chickpeas, rinsed and drained
2 celery stalks, chopped fine
½ red onion, chopped fine
2 tbsp fresh, finely chopped flat-leaf parsley
1 tbsp fresh finely chopped rosemary
90ml/3fl oz/6 tbsp apple cider vinegar
90g/3½ oz/scant ½ cup superfine sugar
60ml/2fl oz/generous ⅜ cup olive oil
salt and pepper

METHOD

In a large bowl, mix the beans, celery, onion, parsley and rosemary.

In a separate small bowl, whisk together the vinegar, sugar, olive oil, salt, and pepper. Add the dressing to the beans. Toss to coat.

Chill beans in the refrigerator for several hours, to allow the beans to soak up the flavor of the dressing.

TOP TIP: CANNED VS DRIED BEANS

Canned beans are quick and easy to use. Alternatively you can prepare dried beans from scratch, however rinse under cold water first to remove any dust or grit, and discard any blemished ones.

- *Overnight Soak:* Cover dried beans with three times their volume of water and let stand in refrigerator for 12 hours or overnight. Drain.

- *Alternative Soak:* In saucepan, cover dried beans with three times their volume of water and bring to boil. Boil for two minutes. Remove from heat, cover and let stand for one hour. Drain.

For greatest economy, cook up a large quantity and freeze in quantities similar to the can sizes you usually use.

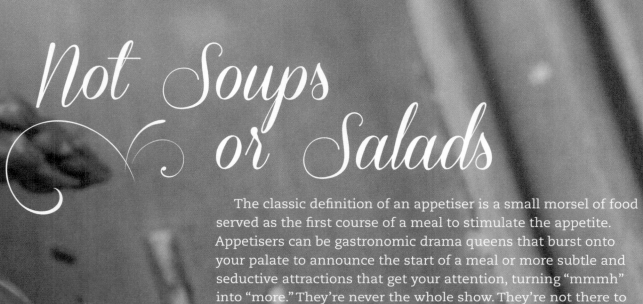

Not Soups
or Salads

The classic definition of an appetiser is a small morsel of food served as the first course of a meal to stimulate the appetite. Appetisers can be gastronomic drama queens that burst onto your palate to announce the start of a meal or more subtle and seductive attractions that get your attention, turning "mmmh" into "more." They're never the whole show. They're not there to fill you up. They're all about getting things started right, whether they're as hands-on as my Sticky Chicken Wings or as highbrow as my Traditional Potted Shrimps, as creamy and soothing as Raglan Risotto or as delicate as Beef Carpaccio. The secret of a great appetiser is this: a lot of taste in a small portion.

SERVES 4-6

Sticky Chicken Wings

Chicken wings are perfect for sharing. I love this particular combination of soy sauce with honey, chilli and ginger and often use this as a marinade for salmon, pork or chicken breasts.

INGREDIENTS

2 tbsp honey
2 tbsp mirin
5 tbsp soy sauce
½ red chilli, finely chopped
1 inch ginger, freshly grated
2 tbsp sunflower oil
14-18 chicken wings
salt and pepper

METHOD

Put the honey, mirin, soy sauce, chilli, ginger and oil into a bowl and mix together. Add in the chicken wings and mix them thoroughly until all of the wings are coated with the sticky glazed mixture. If time allows, leave the wings to marinade overnight, but if you're in more of a rush a couple of hours will suffice.

Preheat the oven to 180°C/350°F/ Gas Mark 4. Arrange the chicken wings on a roasting tray and keep some of the marinade on the side. Season with salt and pepper, then bake for 30-35 minutes until the wings are almost fully cooked.

Meanwhile heat the reserved marinade in a small saucepan and bring to a rapid boil for a moment or two. Careful with it at this stage, as the honey may have a tendency to burn. Sometimes,

if I feel it's reducing too quickly, I add one or two tablespoons of boiled water just to add extra liquid content to the marinade.

After the marinade has come to the boil, pour it over the chicken wings when they come out of the oven and mix it thoroughly with the wings to make sure that, again, they are all coated with the marinade.

Increase the heat of the oven to 200°C/400°F/Gas Mark 6 and return the chicken wings with the marinade to the oven. Allow them to cook for an additional 15-20 minutes. Take them out of the oven every so often and give them a little shake to prevent them from sticking to the tin but also to ensure that each of the wings are covered with the sticky glaze. Serve hot or cold.

Kevin's tip

For variety, try replacing the mirin with dry vermouth or sherry.

SERVES 6-8

Crock of Pâté with Pear & Apricot Chutney

Let's not forget how versatile this tasty treat is – it's luxurious enough to make the table for your festive feasts but is also easy to throw together for lunch all year round. The chutney is the perfect accompaniment, but can be served just on its own with some crusty bread or toast.

INGREDIENTS

25g/1oz/2 tbsp butter
2 tsp oil
2 bacon rashers, finely diced
1 onion, chopped
2 garlic cloves
450g/1lb chicken livers
3 bay leaves
80ml/2¾fl oz/generous
⅓ cup brandy
20ml/¾fl oz/4 tsp cream
130g/4½oz/generous
½ cup butter, softened
seasoning

Pear and apricot chutney
175g/6oz ripe plum
tomatoes, chopped
175g/6oz/⅞ cup superfine sugar
60g/2¼oz cooking apples, diced
60g/2¼oz/scant ½ cup
onions, finely chopped
60g/2¼oz/generous ⅓
cup dried apricots
½ tbsp root ginger, chopped
1 tsp salt
100ml/3½fl oz/scant ½ cup
white wine vinegar
500g/1lb 2oz pears,
diced and chopped

METHOD

Heat the butter in a frying pan with a drizzle of oil, then add the bacon, onion and garlic. Cook gently until softened but not caramelised. Add the chicken livers to the pan with the bay leaves.

Increase the heat and cook for about 3-4 minutes until the livers are nicely browned all over but still pink and soft in the centre. Add the brandy to the livers and flambée. Pour in the cream and simmer for a further 3 minutes, then remove the bay leaves. Pour the mixture into a food processor and blitz it until you get a smooth purée consistency.

Gradually add in the softened butter and season to taste. Spoon the mixture into sterilised jars, then cover with a layer of clarified butter. Store in the fridge until required.

Serve with pear and apricot chutney and some slices of rye bread.

Pear and apricot chutney
Combine all the ingredients except the pears in a large thick-bottomed pan. Simmer uncovered for approximately 1 hour and then add in the diced pears. Stir and continue to simmer until the pears are gently cooked and the consistency is thick and pulpy. Transfer to clean sterilised jars and cover immediately.

Kevin's tip
The chutney needs to be stirred very often to prevent it from sticking to the base of the pot.

To sterilise the jars, place on shelves in the oven (without anything else in the oven) at 280°F/140°C for 20 minutes.

GRAND SOFT DAY?

The Irish climate is renowned for producing a prodigious amount of precipitation. No matter where you are in Ireland, no matter what the season, no day seems complete without its share of the "wet stuff." Despite their day-to-day familiarity with damp surroundings, the Irish retain their ability to express surprise when it rains. There's a phrase the Irish use to describe a constant drizzle or light mist – "a grand soft day." The phrase also can be used ironically when a gale blows in.

How wet is it? Prepare for a surprise. According to the United Nations' "Statistical Yearbook," Ireland was ranked not first, but 50th out of 95 countries for average annual rainfall in their largest cities between 1931 and 1960. That means there were 49 wetter capital cities around the world. Where were they? Were they to be found in exotic, out-of-the-way obscure locations?

Dublin Drier than Rome?

In fact, the rainier cities include Tokyo, London, Berlin and Washington, D.C. Dublin turns out to be drier than Rome. Really! The "dirty auld town" has a mere 29.7 inches of grubby rain a year, while the "eternal city" gets an everlasting 37 inches. Washington, D.C. residents see 10 more inches of rainfall on the White House every year than Dubliners do on Áras an Uachtaráin, official home of Ireland's president. And in Tokyo, the Japanese get nearly double the Dublin drizzle.

Even so, it does rain for between 150 and 225 days of the year across Ireland, with much higher rainfall in the west than in Dublin, but hourly rainfall amounts are low. More like damp drizzle than drenching downpours. So spare a thought for the residents of Conakry in Guinea, West Africa, where nearly 149 inches—that's more than 12 feet of rain—falls every year. Grand soft days, indeed.

"To get enough to eat was regarded as an achievement. To get drunk was a victory."

Brendan Behan (Irish playwright)

Traditional Potted Shrimps

These shrimps are perfect for lunch or an early evening snack, perfect too on brown bread or with a large green salad. In fact, they're just about perfect with most things.

INGREDIENTS

115g/4oz/½ cup butter
(keep 50g/1¾oz/2 tbsp
for clarified butter)
pinch of cayenne pepper
pinch of ground nutmeg
500g/1lb 2oz shrimp
salt and pepper

To serve
Melba toast/crostini bread
1 bunch watercress, washed
1 lemon cut in 4 wedges

METHOD

Put 50g/1¾oz/2 tbsp of butter in a small pan over a low heat to clarify. Leave aside until required.

Place the remaining butter in a pan and melt over a low heat, then add the cayenne pepper and nutmeg. Add the shrimp and cook for 2-3 minutes, stir to combine with the flavoured butter. Season with salt and freshly ground black pepper.

Divide the shrimps between little pots or ramekin dishes and press down gently using the back of a spoon, divide any remaining butter over the shrimps. Top with the clarified butter and chill in the fridge until ready to serve.

Not Soups or Salads   85

SERVES 4

Warm smoked salmon, Confit of Baby Leeks with Lemon Mead Butter

Salmon has long being praised for its taste but also for providing the building blocks of brain cells, so it is crucial to add a bit of salmon to your diet. This genius recipe originated in the Dundon household, where salmon's a favourite.

INGREDIENTS

½ side of smoked salmon
(approximately 400g/14oz)
1 lemon, juiced
2 tbsp mead
200g/7oz/⅞ cup butter, diced
20g/¾oz/2 scant tbsp butter
8 baby leeks, thinly sliced
90ml/3fl oz/6 tbsp white wine
salt and pepper

METHOD

Prepare the smoked salmon by slicing it into thick wedges about 2-3cm/1 inch thick.

To prepare the butter sauce, pour the lemon juice and mead in a small saucepan over a low heat, then add in the diced butter a little at a time and stir gently. Set aside and keep warm.

In a separate pan, melt 20g/¾oz/2 tablespoons butter over a medium heat, then add the chopped leeks and sauté gently for approximately 2 minutes. Pour in the white wine and stir to combine. Add the smoked salmon slices to the pan and season well. Cover and cook for 3-4 minutes until the salmon is heated through.

To serve, place the leeks in the centre of the plate, and then place the salmon on top. Drizzle the lemon mead butter over the salmon and leeks. Serve immediately.

IT STARTED WITH A FISH...

Kilkee, County Clare, Ireland.
Kevin Dundon: Fisherman and Future Chef,
Architect and Restaurateur

One day in the early 1970s while on a family holiday in Kilkee on the West coast of Ireland, young Kevin Dundon went fishing with his father and caught mackerel in the Atlantic Ocean. The family had grilled mackerel that night for dinner, and 6-year-old Kevin decided to cook his grandparents more mackerel for their breakfast the next morning. The fish was not cooked through properly and resembled seared sashimi (Kevin was already precociously ahead of his time). He served it with cold toast. The tea he made was also served cold. He had just cooked his very first meal and, despite its shortcomings, his grandparents were too polite and too fond of their grandson to complain. They ate the meal, and Kevin's career as a chef had begun.

Today, Kevin's choice of ingredients, recipes and culinary presentations often begin with his childhood memories. To understand his food, you first have to know something of his childhood and the family legends passed down to him.

Some of his earliest memories are of stories about his grandfather, who was a surgeon. He was a well-known figure in Limerick and famous for the hats he wore before auctioning them off every year for charity. He had an old-fashioned, almost Victorian attitude about family life, and Kevin's father, Bill Dundon, remembers that, in the family home, the adults ate in the dining room while the children were confined to the kitchen. Bill Dundon happened to glance into the dining room one night when his grandparents were eating their dinner and saw a big bowl of yellow custard on the table. He loved custard and, when his parents had finished their meal and left the room, he went in and took a big dollop of the yellow stuff. Only when it was in his mouth did he realise that it was not custard, but mustard. He has never been able to eat mustard since.

Kevin's mother is English and was brought up in Bulawayo in Rhodesia (now Zimbabwe), before moving back to Great Buckham in Surrey, England when she was 18. Her family also had interesting relatives. King Edward VIII of England was godfather to her grandmother. Kevin's great uncle, James Berryman, was the Minister for Justice during the trial of William Joyce, also known as "Lord Haw Haw," the Irish-American fascist and propagandist infamous for presenting Hitler's Nazi radio broadcasts to Britain during World War II.

"I've got great food memories from his house in Great Buckham as a young kid," Kevin says. Some of the furniture he now has in Dunbrody House hails from the family house in Great Buckham, including the gong used to summon the family to breakfast, lunch and dinner. The food, he recalls, was served from Victorian side stations and was prepared by Mrs. Gallagher, the Irish cook who was, in his own words, "grumpy as hell. My sister, Sharon, and I used to always be under her feet."

Kevin was born in Dublin after his parents moved back to Ireland. His grandmother and his mother both had a real passion for food that he remembers vividly from his childhood. They were so passionate that, when the Dundon family were eating dinner in the evening, they would already be discussing and planning the menu for the following night! "Because Mum was brought up in Rhodesia," Kevin explains, "we were eating much more varied and exciting food than my friends would eat." Dishes such as Peri Peri Chicken and Lasagne were considerably more exotic compared to what was eaten in most Irish homes in the 1970s.

Kevin was expected to follow his father's footsteps and have a career in medicine but, after his parents split up, he rebelled. Whatever his father decided he should do, Kevin decided to do the complete opposite. He really wanted to be an architect but, unfortunately, his Dad really liked that idea. So Kevin put his love of architecture on the back burner and decided to pursue a culinary path, instead. "Cooking and architecture are similar," he says. "Both are artistic, and I do get a huge amount of buzz from the architectural work I've done on Dunbrody House."

His first job was at the Hollybrook Hotel in Clontarf, Dublin where he wanted to be a chef. When a kitchen porter's job came up, he took it just so he could watch the cooks. He got his first chance as chef in The Old Schoolhouse restaurant in Swords, Dublin, and continued his studies at Dublin College of Catering, graduating there in 1986.

"What I also liked about cooking was that it gave me great opportunities to travel," Kevin says.

Kevin won a scholarship to work at the prestigious La Mère Catherine restaurant in Zurich, Switzerland, but soon discovered that the regimen at his boarding house was not to his liking.

"We were given digs that we couldn't eat in, couldn't make any noise in after 10 p.m., and we had to be up by 8 a.m., even on days off, because the landlady used to just walk into my room without knocking and start cleaning it." Kevin used his trademark creativity to solve the problem. "I set my alarm for 7:45 a.m., stripped off bollock naked and simply lay there on the bed when she walked in. She always knocked after that," he says.

His mother, drawing on her own experience of life in Africa, impressed on Kevin that travel would be the best education he would ever get. So when he saw that Wind Star Sails were advertising for chefs on one of their cruise liners, he applied for and got the job. He was soon working 16 hours a day, seven days a week and found that he enjoyed it. He especially liked working on the larger ships that would stop at small ports and bring in fresh lobsters or crayfish that he would serve that night. "It was all about the fresh, natural ingredients."

His next position was as sous chef at Fairmont Hotels & Resorts Canada where he represented Canada in culinary competitions. Kevin also completed his master's degree in Canada and received honours in "chef de cuisine" in 1992. "I then started to concentrate on my career as a chef because, even at that point, I was still thinking of switching to architecture." He ended up spending more than seven and a half years in Canada. The job was daunting, but the company had supported and believed in him, and Kevin felt he had to repay that trust with culinary excellence.

Kevin had already met his future wife, Catherine, when he was age 17 and they both lived in Dublin. Because Kevin spent long periods away from Ireland, it was an on-and-off relationship. But in 1992, the couple became engaged while on a skiing holiday, and they married in 1994. They now have three children: Emily, Sophie and Tom. For some time, they considered where they might settle down.

"I always said that I would only move home to Ireland for the position of executive chef at the (five-star) Shelbourne or Dromoland Castle, or to open my own place," Kevin explains.

They were heading for their honeymoon in Portugal and were at Dublin Airport when their plane was delayed. "Catherine bought a copy of the Irish Independent and, lo and behold, they were advertising the job of executive chef in The Shelbourne." Kevin applied, got the job and filled the highly esteemed post for two years.

It was while he was there that Dunbrody House entered his life. "Any time I got stressed, I would walk around St. Stephen's Green in Dublin to cool down. I was walking past an estate agent's window in 1996, and I saw houses similar to Dunbrody House for sale at reasonable prices."

At the time, the start of the housing boom that accompanied the Celtic Tiger Years of rapid economic growth had not spread beyond Dublin, and Kevin felt that it was worth a trip to Wexford to look at some properties. The moment he and Catherine entered Dunbrody House, even though it had been closed for 15 years, they knew it was right for them.

Dunbrody House Hotel and Restaurant is now considered one of Ireland's premier establishments and has won numerous awards including Irish Restaurant of the Year in 2004, 2005 and 2006, driven by Kevin's innovative Irish cuisine and his passion for cooking. Opening the restaurant meant that he could go back to what he likes best – spending time in the kitchen.

"I love to cook but, the more successful I became in my career, the less cooking I did. When I opened the restaurant at Dunbrody, I was back in the kitchen every night. I was in my element," he says. Kevin was also able to revive and draw on his love of architecture when restoring the house and grounds.

A side career in the media soon followed after Kevin opened Dunbrody House.

"A place like Dunbrody House is a big beast, and it takes money to keep it going to a very high standard. Journalists used to come down here all the time and when they asked me would I do a TV show for them I thought why not?" As well as being a regular on Irish radio, Kevin also has appeared on numerous television networks including ESPN Cable, NBC, the BBC, CBC (Live) Canada, RTE (Live) Ireland and "No Frontiers" travel show.

The appearances on U.S. television networks came about after Kevin met John Cooke, one of the other two owners of Raglan Road. John told Kevin that the Irish Pub Company was opening Nine Fine Irishmen in Las Vegas for MGM, and they were looking for a consultant. John wanted Kevin to provide a menu of modern Irish cuisine and to supply one of the Irish Pub Company's Five Fundamentals – good Irish food.

"John came down to Dunbrody. It was a winter's night, the kitchen was closed, but John was hungry, so I cooked up two dinners for ourselves and listened to him explain the concept. I said I'd go and have a look."

Kevin went to Las Vegas to assist with Nine Fine Irishmen and discovered that he, John Cooke and Paul Nolan, the third of the trio of Irish owners of Raglan Road, really got on well together. "We shared a passion for portraying Ireland as it really is and not just an impression of what people think Ireland is like," Kevin says.

That shared vision would ultimately result in their becoming owner-partners of Raglan Road, the first Irish pub in the United States to be Irish owned, Irish managed and authentically Irish in its design, cuisine, entertainment and beverages. But before we learn how Raglan Road was conceived and created, we stop on our journey to spend a little more time with young Kevin to see how his childhood memories shape his culinary philosophy today.

THE FOOD OF MEMORIES

Dunbrody House, County Wexford, Ireland.
Kevin Dundon: Chef

"When you live in Ireland, you don't really appreciate how good our natural ingredients are here. It's all about the true flavour of the Irish food—about sourcing good natural raw ingredients and letting them speak for themselves. I think that's what I really learned from the years I spent traveling outside of Ireland."

We take a well-earned rest on the road to Raglan Road to learn about Chef Kevin Dundon's unique take on Irish cuisine, in his own words. He starts, as always, with memories of his childhood.

"I always remember going into my Auntie Joyce's larder in her country house when I was young, and there would be rows and rows of jam jars, each one full with pickled chutneys and jams that she'd made herself. Well, that stuck with me.

"I do a Sinful Trifle with Swiss Roll—Swiss Roll is another favourite of mine from childhood—sliced roll with fruit and custard and sherry. When it came to serving it up, I decided to put it in a jam jar, so now it's a jam jar of trifle. That dish, for me, combines the feel of an old country house with my childhood memories and innovative presentation.

"If you look at my Sticky Toffee Pudding, it's about textures—the richness of the dates inside and the smooth creamy custard on top. Everybody loves that food because it's classic childhood comfort food."

Kevin loves the way Raglan Road enables him to express the playful and creative side of his cuisine.

"The contrast between Dunbrody House in Ireland and Raglan Road in the United States is that I can play a lot more with Raglan Road. It's the same quality ingredients but mad ideas and off-the-wall, really creative presentation.

"Bacon and cabbage, I think, is one of the best dishes you can eat in the world. To make it a little different, I do a loin of bacon with an Irish mist and a honey glaze on Colcannon potato cake. Here, I'm taking a traditional Irish dish and giving it a twist to make it more contemporary without losing its Irish roots.

"Roast rack of lamb and Irish jus consommé is about showing how Irish food can be made more sophisticated. American guests at Raglan Road are often surprised at how modern Irish cuisine has developed in Ireland over the past 25 years.

"Take something as simple as fish and chips, which every Irish person knows from the thousands of local chippers around Ireland. I looked at fish and chips and came up with a tempura beer batter that is extremely crispy and gets golden brown for our fresh haddock. But it was an absolute nightmare to plate up! I always have visions of my childhood when coming up with new concepts. I remembered leaning up against a wall somewhere eating fresh battered fish and chips straight out of newspaper. Wouldn't it be great if I could recreate that? But you simply can't do that in a busy restaurant, so I came up with the idea to make a cone out of newspaper for the fish to stand up in, instead.

"Sausages and battered sausages served in Irish pubs are good 'soakage' (food of average quality eaten as an accompaniment to drink), but I like traditional food. How could I make them work in Raglan Road? I said we had to do what I called a Forest of Forks. We had boards made and stuck forks into them standing tines up, then stuck sausages onto them so you could eat them easily without fuss or mess. Just pick up a fork and away you go.

"These concepts come from the practical side of how things can be eaten. I sit at a stool in a bar, then ask myself what would I like to eat and how would I like to eat it. I'm that hands on. Dishes do not have to be complicated as long as they taste great.

"A simple roast chicken, for example, is spectacular when it's cooked correctly. Chefs in Ireland have a habit of skipping steps to move things along quicker. When making soups, they might chuck everything in at once instead of heating the pan, cooking the butter then frying the onion for five minutes in it, and so on. Taking the time to get the basics right is the best way to ensure good results every time.

"The 'Dunbrody Kiss' is a bit more sophisticated because I created it for Dunbrody House as a signature dish. I've changed it up and made it into a 'Jaffa Kiss,' so it's going back to childhood memories again, this time of the 'Jaffa Cake' biscuits that Irish children love. The dish has got sponge at the bottom, an orange marmalade filling, chocolate truffle mousse over the top. And it's covered in chocolate ganache. It's a very rich and comforting dessert and immediately takes me back to being a kid.

"There are certain Raglan Road recipes that I just cannot take off the menu. I know—I've tried! The 'Smokie City' appetizer for sharing mixes smoked haddock, chopped tomato, Dubliner cheese and cream and is baked in the oven. I sometimes get bored and want to change things up a little but, when I took it off the menu, there was uproar, and it had to go back on!

"There's one dish, a Tomato and Gin soup that Raglan Road guests loved, and we occasionally feature as the soup of the day. People started to call the restaurant just to find out if it was on that day and to schedule their visits accordingly. It had to go full time on the menu.

"The look and feel of Raglan Road also has an influence on how I approach the food. The Raglan Road Room is paneled in wood reclaimed from Irish houses of the Victorian era and has the feel of a Gentlemen's Club, which takes me back to the Savoy Grill in London where I remember being taken as a child and seeing the waiters going up the aisle with a carvery. For that reason, I did a carved suckling pig for one of our four signature dinners that we do every year. The Music Room, to me, has more of a bistro feel. The Grand Room is the life and soul of the pub, so there has to be a fun element to the food we offer there."

While keeping it fun for Raglan Road guests, Kevin also is meticulous about his food's authenticity and attention to detail.

"I won't use any fish that is not from the Atlantic Ocean because that's the sea that surrounds Ireland. No rock lobster from the Caribbean will ever appear on the menu. With our bread, I won't let them use a mixer because, when you use a mixer, the dough gets too tight. When we're doing at least 1,200 covers every day, it makes it hard doing it by hand but it keeps it authentic.

"How do I decide the menu? We just cook for days, non-stop, trying dishes out, tasting everything. My main chef will come over to Ireland for a week, and together we will work on my future vision for Raglan Road. At the moment, I'm going back to the classics. Dishes like Steak Diane, Coquille St. Jacques, Knickerbocker Glories, but all smartly done and innovatively presented."

SERVES 4

Beef Carpaccio

It's a must to use a decent, sharp knife for this recipe or you'll find that you end up with beef slices that are thick, lumpy and uneven rather than thin and elegant. Trust me, you want thin and elegant every time!

INGREDIENTS

250g/9oz beef fillet
(you'll need a nice thick
piece of centre cut)
2 egg yolks
100ml/3½fl oz/scant ½ cup
extra virgin olive oil
1 lemon, juiced
½ tsp English mustard
salt and pepper
a handful of arugula leaves
Parmesan cheese, shaved
with a potato peeler
Maldon salt

METHOD

Put the beef into the freezer for 30 minutes to firm it up, which will make it easier to slice.

Meanwhile, to make the dressing, put the egg yolks in a bowl and whisk, slowly, adding the olive oil in a steady stream. Season with lemon juice, mustard, salt and pepper and mix well.

Take the beef out of the freezer. Using a very sharp, large knife, cut slices as thinly as you can. Lay these on a plate and cover them with clingfilm as you cut to stop them colouring. A layer of baking parchment or clingfilm between the individual layers also means you'll easily be able to separate them out later.

To serve, plate the beef slices on a platter or individual plates, heap some arugula leaves in the middle and drizzle the dressing around the edge. Finish with a scattering of Parmesan shavings and crushed Maldon salt.

SERVES 4

Scallop Forest with Lime Mayonnaise

This makes a wonderful starter for a dinner party, but feel free to enjoy any time the mood strikes!

INGREDIENTS

12 fresh scallops,
coral removed
100g/3½oz/1 scant cup
plain flour seasoned
with salt and pepper

Batter
300g/10½oz/generous
2½ cups, firmly packed
plain flour
100g/3½oz/generous
⅔ cup cornflour
200ml/7fl oz/generous
¾ cup soda water
1½ cups/12fl oz/350ml
lager (Harp or Budweiser)
salt and pepper

Lime mayonnaise
250g/9oz mayonnaise
3 limes, zest and juice
1 tbsp chives, fresh snipped

METHOD

To make the lime mayonnaise, place the mayonnaise in a bowl and add the lime juice and zest, combine well and refrigerate until required.

In a large bowl, sift in the flour, cornflour, salt and pepper. Pour in the lager and soda water and whisk until you've got a smooth batter. Allow to rest at room temperature for about 30 minutes.

Preheat a deep fat fryer to 180°C/350°F/Gas Mark 4. Dredge the scallops in flour to coat, then shake off the excess flour. Dip the scallops in the batter, then shake to remove excess.

Carefully place the scallops in the hot oil. Cook for about 4-5 minutes until golden. Remove from the oil and place on kitchen paper to drain, then season with salt and pepper. Serve immediately with the lime mayonnaise.

Smoked Salmon Platter

*Wasabi gives the crème fraiche a real kick up the backside,
so use it sparingly!*

INGREDIENTS

16 slices smoked salmon,
thinly sliced

Wasabi crème fraiche
250ml/9fl oz/generous
1 cup crème fraîche
2 tsp chopped parsley
½ lemon or lime, juice only
½ tsp wasabi
cracked black pepper

Bloody tomato sorbet
150ml/5fl oz/⅔ cup
tomato juice
20g/¾oz/4 tsp superfine sugar
100ml/3½fl oz/scant
½ cup passata
90ml/3fl oz/6 tbsp vodka
6 dashes Worcestershire sauce
½ lemon, juice only
3 dashes Tabasco sauce
pinch salt and pepper

METHOD

To make the sorbet, combine the tomato juice, sugar, passata, vodka and Worcestershire sauce in a liquidiser and blend until smooth. Pour the contents into a large bowl and stir in the lemon juice, Tabasco and seasoning.

Next, pour the ingredients into an ice cream maker and churn until it's the consistency of a sorbet. Freeze until required.

In the meantime, place the crème fraîche, parsley, lemon juice, wasabi and cracked black pepper in a bowl, and using a wooden spoon gently combine the ingredients together.

To serve, place the smoked salmon on a serving dish, add a small quenelle of the wasabi crème fraiche, and a shot of bloody Mary sorbet. Serve immediately.

Coconut & Curry Crock of Mussels

Everyone loves a bowl of steaming fragrant mussels. They should be fat, juicy and bursting with flavour. I've added curry paste and coconut milk to give this bowl of mussels a spicy Asian twist.

INGREDIENTS

1kg/2lb 4oz mussels, scrubbed
1 tbsp olive oil
1 onion, finely diced
1 garlic clove, thinly sliced
splash of wine
200ml/7fl oz/generous
¾ cup coconut milk
1-2 tsp Thai curry paste
½ lemon, juice only
salt and pepper
fresh parsley, to garnish
1 lime, cut into wedges

METHOD

Drizzle some olive oil in a pan and add the diced onions and garlic. Sauté gently for 2-3 minutes until translucent but not browned.

Toss the mussels into the pan over a high heat, and add a splash of wine to cook them. Cover and continue to cook for a further 2–3 minutes until the mussels are open, shaking the pan every now and then to diffuse the heat. Remove any unopened mussels at this stage and discard.

Pour the coconut milk over the mussels, spoon in the curry paste and cook for 2 minutes. Add a handful of fresh parsley and stir gently over a low heat.

Serve in a large bowl with a wedge of lime and some crusty bread.

SERVES 4

Calamari City

This light batter gives the calamari a wonderful new dimension. Tempura vegetables can be the perfect vegetarian option. Spice up the mayo with some chilli flakes instead of lime!

INGREDIENTS

500g/1lb 2oz calamari,
cut into 5mm/¼ inch rings
2-5 courgette flowers
1 carrot, cut into strips
40g/1½oz/5tbsp plain
flour, seasoned
salt and pepper

Tempura batter
175g/6oz/1½ cups, firmly
packed plain flour
½ tsp smoked paprika
½ tsp cayenne pepper
½ tsp bread soda
50g/1¾oz/generous
1/3 cup cornflour
½ tsp salt
250ml/9fl oz/generous
1 cup sparkling water
vegetable oil, for deep frying

Lime mayonnaise
250g/9oz mayonnaise
3 limes, zest and juice
1 tbsp chives, fresh snipped

METHOD

Preheat the deep fat fryer to 180°C/350°F. To ensure the oil is at the correct temperature, drop a cube of bread into it–it should become golden within 1 minute.

Meanwhile, sift the flour, cornflour, paprika, cayenne pepper and bread soda into a bowl and add the salt. Pour in the sparkling water and stir using a whisk to create a batter.

Coat the calamari and vegetables in a little seasoned flour, then shake to remove any excess. Dip the floured calamari and vegetables into the batter. Place the calamari and vegetables in the preheated deep fat fryer and cook for 2-3 minutes until golden.

Remove from the oil and drain on kitchen paper, season with salt and pepper and serve with a big dollop of lime mayonnaise.

Lime mayonnaise
To make the lime mayonnaise, place the mayonnaise in a bowl and add the lime juice and zest, combine well and refrigerate until required.

SERVES 4

Raglan Risotto

When preparing this dish, it's important that your chicken stock stays hot at all times before being added to the dish. Otherwise, it will cool the risotto down during cooking and that'll make it very stodgy (not a good thing).

INGREDIENTS

350g/12oz/generous 1½ cups arborio/carnaroli rice
25g/1oz/2 tbsp butter
2 shallots, peeled and finely diced
½ tsp fresh thyme
200g/7oz wild mushrooms
3 garlic cloves, very finely diced
150ml/5fl oz/⅔ cup dry white wine
1 litre/1¾ pints/scant 4½ cups boiling chicken or vegetable stock
100g/3½oz/scant ½ cup mascarpone
75g/2¾oz/scant ¾ cup freshly grated Parmesan cheese
150g/5oz/1½ cups green peas (optional)
salt and pepper

METHOD

Choose a wide saucepan with a thick base. On a low heat, slowly melt the butter and add the chopped shallots, thyme, wild mushrooms and garlic and cook very gently until completely softened. Add the arborio rice and mix well to ensure that it does not stick to the base of the pan at this crucial time.

Allow the rice to become glazed and cook without any liquid for 3-4 minutes whilst continuing to stir at all times (ensuring that the heat remains low). Next, add in the white wine and, again, continue to stir the rice because the wine will evaporate off quite quickly. Add some boiling chicken or vegetable stock into the rice.

Add the stock, little by little, never adding the next ladle until the previous one has evaporated. It is vitally important not to rush this process but continue to add all of the liquid until the rice is plump and tender at about the 18-20 minute mark. Season well. If you want a nice creamy risotto, add the mascarpone now.

Serve immediately with additional Parmesan cheese and a few green peas (if you want to add a little colour and sweetness to the dish).

Asparagus & Goat Cheese Tartlet

Served warm or cold, these are sure to please. Replace the asparagus with some red onion marmalade for another flavoursome variation.

INGREDIENTS

20g/¾oz/1 generous
tbsp butter
2 leeks, thinly sliced
50ml/1¾fl oz/scant
¼ cup cream
12 spears of asparagus,
cut in half lengthways
400g/14oz Boilie goat cheese
salt and pepper

Pastry
250g/9oz/2¼ cups, firmly
packed plain flour
125g/4½oz/generous
½ cup butter
pinch of salt
1 egg

METHOD

Preheat the oven to 180°C/350°F/ Gas Mark 4. Prepare the shortcrust pastry by sifting the flour into a bowl and adding the butter and salt. Use your fingertips to combine the ingredients until the mix resembles breadcrumbs. Add in the egg and use a knife to mix. The pastry should come together into a ball. Roll out the pastry and cut to fit your tartlet dish or dishes. Pre-bake in the oven for 12 minutes.

In a medium-sized pan, add the butter, let it melt and then add the chopped leeks. Sauté for 5 minutes on a medium heat, then add the cream and seasoning and cook for a further 2-3 minutes to reduce the cream.

In the meantime, place a large pot of hot water to boil with salt. Prepare a bowl of ice cold water on the side. When boiling, place carefully the asparagus in the water and simmer for 2-4 minutes depending on the size of the asparagus. Remove from the water with a spider or in a colander and place in the ice cold water. This will stop the cooking of the asparagus, keeping them green and crunchy.

Fill the pre-baked tart with the creamed leek, then place the asparagus spears on top, add the goat cheese on top of them.

Place the tartlet in the oven for 10-15 minutes to allow the cheese enough time to melt and caramelise. Serve with fresh leaves.

SERVES 4

Scallops St. Jacques

Scallops can be eaten raw or cooked. They can be sliced up raw, then drizzled with a little truffle oil for a simple carpaccio. In this recipe, I cook the scallops in wine and serve them with duchesse potatoes and a Mornay sauce using the scallop shells as dishes.

INGREDIENTS

12 scallops, coral removed
150ml/5fl oz/⅔ cup fish stock
150ml/5fl oz/⅔ cup white wine
½ leek, thinly sliced
1 tbsp melted butter

Duchesse potatoes
500g/1lb 2oz potatoes
85g/3oz/⅜ cup butter
large pinch of grated nutmeg
50ml/1¾fl oz/scant ¼ cup cream
3 egg yolks
salt

Mornay sauce
65g/2⅓ oz/scant 5 tbsp butter
35g/1¼oz/4 tbsp plain flour
500ml/17fl oz/generous
2 cups milk
50g/1¾oz/½ cup cheddar
cheese, grated
2 egg yolks
salt and pepper

4 large scallops shells or shallow individual baking dishes to serve.

METHOD

Preheat the oven to 200°C/400°F/ Gas Mark 6. Place the scallop shells on a baking tray using either slices of bread or a bed of scrunched-up foil to prevent them from tipping over.

Place the potatoes in a pan and barely cover with water. Boil until tender. Strain any excess liquid from the potatoes, then add the butter, cream, nutmeg and salt. Mash until smooth. Return the pan to a low heat and using a wooden spoon, stir in the egg yolks, adjust seasoning as necessary. Allow the potatoes to cool slightly, then spoon into a piping bag and pipe a generous border of potato around the edge of each scallop shell.

Heat the fish stock and wine in a pan, then add the scallops. Cover and lightly poach for 1–2 minutes until just beginning to whiten (the scallops will continue to cook further in the sauce even when removed from the heat). Remove the scallops from the liquid and set aside.

To cook the leeks, place a knob of butter in a pan and when foaming add the leeks. Cook for 2–3 minutes until softened, then season well. Place the leeks in the base of the scallop shells.

For the sauce, melt the butter in a saucepan. When it begins to sizzle, add the flour and cook the roux, stirring continuously. Be careful not to let it brown. Pour the milk into the roux and whisk vigorously. Bring the sauce to the boil, then reduce the heat and stir in the grated cheese. Remove from the heat, then add in the egg yolk until you get a creamy consistency. Season with salt and freshly ground black pepper.

Place the scallops on the bed of leeks in the potato edged shell, then spoon some of the mornay sauce over the scallop and leeks. Bake until browned and bubbling for roughly 12-15 minutes. Serve immediately.

SERVES 4

Smoked Haddock Smokey

Try to use naturally smoked haddock as opposed to dyed fish. Alternatively, you can substitute haddock for any firm smoked fish such as cod or coley.

INGREDIENTS

1 tbsp olive oil
500g/1lb 2oz naturally
smoked haddock, skin
removed and diced
1 large potato, diced
into small cubes
1 punnet (200g/7oz)
cherry tomatoes, halved
3 spring onions
125ml/4fl oz/generous
½ cup crème fraiche
200ml/7fl oz/generous
¾ cup cream
115g/4oz/1 cup mature
Cheddar cheese, grated

METHOD

Pre-heat your oven to 180°C/
350°F/Gas Mark 4/Gas Mark 4.

Heat a large frying pan with
1 tablespoon of oil and fry the
haddock pieces for approximately
2 minutes. Add the potato,
tomatoes, spring onions, crème
fraiche and cream and cook for a
further 8-10 minutes on a lower
simmering heat. Remove from
the heat. Season lightly and add
half of the cheese to melt in the
infused cream.

Divide the mixture between
4 ramekin dishes or crock
pots. Sprinkle the top with the
cheddar cheese and place in the
oven until the cheese is bubbling
and slightly browned.

Serve immediately with some
nice crusty bread or a salad.

WE NEED TO TALK ABOUT CUISINE

Ireland.
The Irish: A Hungry People

Irish families became dependent on the potato for their survival—tragically dependent, as it turned out. The road to Raglan Road would not be complete without a mention of Irish cuisine, which splits neatly into two eras. BP (Before Potatoes) and AP (After Potatoes). What did Irish people eat before the modern era, and is there such a thing as Irish cuisine?

What we think of today as traditional Irish cuisine—foods like soda bread, barm brack, boxty, champ, colcannon, Irish stew and coddle—were not what ordinary Irish people would have eaten in the distant past. These dishes were more likely to have been enjoyed by the wealthier farming class after the introduction of the potato. To understand what was really eaten in most Irish homes, we need to go back to a time before these famously Irish foodstuffs became popularised.

BP, Before Potatoes, most Irish people cooked their meals in a pot or cauldron suspended over a fire that was always kept hot. What went into the pot depended on where you lived and whether you could easily forage for food there. If you lived near the coast, crabs, lobsters, fish, other shellfish and seaweed formed the basis of most meals, which were served as a soup or broth. Inland, Irish cooks might cook a sheep's head in the cauldron. Birds and even hedgehogs were cooked by covering them in clay then baking them in fires. When cooked through, the baked clay was smashed and the animals plucked or skinned, then eaten. Fish could be cooked by roasting them on spits. Other more unusual animals caught and eaten included badgers, seals and porpoises, which were known as "sea pigs."

Most families were able to keep a few actual pigs or sheep, so mutton, lamb and pork formed a small part of their diet, with the meat being salted to preserve it for the days ahead. Bread was made from oats, with the dough being placed in the cauldron overnight so that it would rise. Scones were cooked on hot coals with the mixture wrapped in cabbage leaves, and sheep's cheeses were made using rennet, a complex of enzymes obtained from sheep's stomach. Wild birds' eggs were gathered and fried on hot stones. Goose eggs were considered a delicacy and eaten at Easter or Midsummer's Day. The technique of collecting blood from healthy cattle without harming them, mixing it with meal and making blood pudding, also known as black pudding, was widespread across Ireland.

One of the most famous Irish legends concerns the cooking of fish. In it, Finegas, a poet, spent seven years fishing for a salmon thought to contain all the world's knowledge. On finally catching the fish, he gave it to his servant Fionn to cook, with strict instructions not to eat any of it. Fionn cooked the salmon without eating it but, when he pressed his thumb against it to see if it was cooked, he burned it on a drop of fish fat. He sucked his thumb to relieve the pain and all the world's knowledge was transferred into Fionn in an instant. Fionn went on to become leader of the Fianna, a band of Irish mythical heroes.

AP, After Potatoes, the Irish population divided into the richer families who owned more than 10 acres of land and the poorer ones, the majority, who had less. For the poor, the potato meant that they could more easily feed themselves on a small plot of land, especially during the winter months. To add to the main dish of potatoes, they grew cabbage and kale. For the rich, who were able to buy meat, fish and breads, the potato became the main vegetable in most meals. Consequently, while the rich were able to adapt, the potato famine of the mid-18th century caused widespread starvation among the poor.

Today's Irish Cuisine

Today, Ireland enjoys an abundance of high-quality fresh produce including vegetables, fruits and grains supported by a temperate climate. It is a country rich in seafood and with vast grazing land for cattle. Contemporary Irish cuisine is based on good, fresh local produce with few supporting ingredients. The food speaks for itself without heavy sauces or hot spices. Recipes tend to be simple and easily followed in homes across the country. It is a cuisine suited more for family meals than for fine restaurants.

These rich natural ingredients set the stage for a new generation of creative Irish chefs to bring new Irish cuisine to the world's attention. For one young Irish chef, like Fionn in the legend, it began with a fish—a fish that inspired him to cook his very first meal.

Mains

The appetisers set the stage, the desserts bring the curtain down, but the main course is the heart and soul of the show. We've reached the red meat of the story of the Road to Raglan Road, a tale that crossed the globe, stopped for a pint, and finally found its way to America. As with any great dish, the best way to approach this section is to get stuck in it straight away.

Red Meat

This is the good stuff. After the delicacy of the soups and salads and the lightness of the appetisers' touch come the full-on mains. Here's where you'll find my recipes for hearty dishes like my Striploin of Beef with marmalade butter & pomme pont-neuf, my Whole Glazed Ham and my Roasted Leg of Lamb with herb crust. Sounds daunting? Well, preparing and cooking large joints of meat doesn't have to be complicated. I show you how to master the dish step by step. Not all the recipes are for big barnstorming meals. My Lamb Pasta Ragout and Curry Beef Pie are great, comforting everyday meals for all the family.

SERVES 8 – 10

Kevin's Whole Glazed Ham

Pork, ham and bacon are undoubtedly the meats that most people associate with Irish cooking. Ham is simply pork that has been cured and sometimes smoked to give it a lively, mildly spiced taste. True ham starts out as the pig's hind leg, which is then either wet or dry-cured. Here's my recipe for glazed ham with a whiskey twist.

INGREDIENTS

whole ham on the bone
(approximately 3.5kg/7lb 8oz)
18 cloves
50g/1¾oz/¼ cup, solidly
packed brown sugar
4 tbsp apricot preserve
4 tbsp Irish Mist
whiskey liqueur

METHOD

Soak the ham first for up to 1 hour. Time to nip down to the pub or to finally start reading James Joyce's epic novel Ulysses! Good luck.

Put into a pot, cover with water and bring to the boil. Allow to simmer for about 2 hours, then turn off the heat, allowing the meat to cool in the cooking liquor.

Remove the ham from the cooking liquor and using a sharp knife remove the rind, leaving an even layer of fat. Score diamond shaped lines into the fat, then stud the cloves into the layer of fat and put onto a baking tray.

To make the glaze mix the sugar, apricot preserve and Irish Mist whiskey together until well combined. Spread this over the clove-studded ham.

Loosely cover with tin foil and bake in the oven at 150°C/300°F/ Gas Mark 2 for about an hour or perhaps a little more, depending largely on your oven.

Remove tin foil at this stage and turn up the heat for an additional 20 minutes until browned.

Rest the meat for an additional 30 minutes out of the oven before slicing.

Kevin's tip
I prefer to cook my ham by placing it in a pot and bringing it to the boil, then simmering for 2–2½ hours before putting into the oven to bake for the final hour, but if you prefer to bake your ham from the start here are my recommendations.

After allowing the ham to soak in water for at least 2–4 hours, pat dry and place ham fat side up on a rack in a shallow baking pan and add a little water under the rack – cover with foil and bake for the following times. Remember to remove the foil for the last half-hour.

Cooking times
3.5–4.5kg/8–10lb around 3½ hours
4.5–5.5kg/10–12lb around 3½ to 4 hours
5.5–6.75kg/12–15lb around 4 to 4½ hours
6.75–8kg/15–18lb around 4½ to 5 hours
8–10kg/18–22lb around 5 to 6 hours
10–10/75kg/22–24lb around 6 to 6½ hours

Another tip
Hams are sold with or without the bone. To determine the correct amount to buy, estimate needing 350g/12oz of bone-in ham per person, or 115g/4oz of boneless ham per person.

And another
When you freeze ham, you take away from the quality of the meat so eat it fresh when you can. You can store tightly wrapped left over ham in the refrigerator for up to 4 days. If you do want to freeze it, wrap tightly and do not freeze over two months. Alternatively you can turn any leftovers into a savoury pea and ham soup then freeze the soup!

And yet another tip
Baking with glaze will add more flavour and help keep the meat moist; it's not necessary to do but it does add a nice touch.
Do not baste ham in its own juices when baking, as this will make the joint too salty.

Glazed Loin of Bacon with Colcannon Mash

The shape of loin of bacon is perfect for easy carving and it makes a nice change from traditional ham.

INGREDIENTS

Glazed loin of bacon
900g/2lb loin of bacon
2 tbsp Irish Mist
whiskey liqueur
4 tbsp honey
100ml/3½fl oz/scant
½ cup cider

Colcannon Mash
8 small Savoy cabbage leaves,
trimmed down to form cups
5–6 large potatoes, peeled
55g/2oz/¼ cup butter
60ml/2fl oz/generous
⅜ cup buttermilk
100g/3½oz Savoy
cabbage, shredded
salt and pepper

METHOD

Place the loin of bacon in a large pan and cover with cold water. Bring to the boil, then reduce the heat and simmer for 1 hour until completely tender.

Preheat the oven to 180°C/150°F/ Gas Mark 4. Place the Irish Mist in a pan with the honey and cider, then heat gently until dissolved. Remove the loin of bacon from the water and leave until cool enough to handle, then trim away the rind and excess fat.

Place the loin of bacon in a small roasting tin and brush all over with the glaze, pouring any remainder around the loin. Bake for 15-20 minutes until completely heated through and well glazed, basting occasionally.

Remove the bacon from the oven and leave in a warm place for at least 10 minutes. Blanch the cabbage cups in a pan of boiling salted water until just tender but still holding their shape. Drain well and toss in the remaining knob of butter. Season to taste.

Meanwhile bring the potatoes to the boil, then simmer for 15-20 minutes or until completely tender. Drain in a colander and return to the saucepan. Add the butter and buttermilk, then mash using a potato masher. Add the shredded cabbage and season well with salt and pepper.

Slice the bacon and place on a bed of colcannon mash, and the Savoy cabbage cups and drizzle with pan reduction.

Serve immediately or sooner.

FROM CONQUISTADORS TO CONNACHT

Potatoes and Ireland—the two seem inextricably linked. Some people think potatoes are native to Ireland, yet the vegetable was not introduced here until about 400 years ago.

Potatoes or "papas" were found originally only in Peru and Chile. The Spanish conquistadors, who came to the New World seeking gold, were the first Europeans to discover them in South America and thought the potato was a kind of truffle. Soon after, they discovered that sailors who ate them on board their ships did not develop scurvy. Consequently, potatoes became popular, and the Spanish began serving them as a dish.

Nobody knows exactly how the first potato reached Ireland. Sir Walter Raleigh is thought to have brought potatoes to his estates in Youghal, County Cork, in 1588. Legend has it that he made a gift of the potato to Queen Elizabeth I of England. Raleigh also tried to grow tobacco brought back from Virginia. The potato crop flourished, but the tobacco failed. Had the situation been reversed, the history of Ireland would have been very different.

Another story is that the first potatoes washed ashore on the West of Ireland from the sunken ships of the Spanish Armada—the ships carrying Spanish forces to invade England—in 1588. The story is supported by the fact that the potato was often referred to in the West as the Spaniard.

Tragedy in the growing

By the 1780s, the Irish had adopted the new and nutritious potato and quickly came to rely on it. Unlike existing crops, it could be grown easily without much cultivation and feed up to 10 people from just one acre of land.

It was this very heavy dependence on potatoes for food that made the blight of 1845 and beyond so devastating in Ireland. The fungus first was detected in Mexico, made its way to North America and then to Europe by the middle of the 18th century. Other European countries, notably Belgium and Scotland, suffered similarly dramatic losses in their potato harvest. But nowhere was the crop planted as widely as in Ireland, where starvation was widespread.

"We have always found the Irish to be a bit odd. They refuse to be English."

Winston Churchill (British politician)

Baby Back Pork Ribs with Guinness Reduction & Potato Salad

Ribs and Guinness – a match made in heaven!

INGREDIENTS

1.5kg/3lb 5oz rack
Baby Pork Ribs
300ml/10fl oz/1¼ cups
dry cider (good quality)
5 fennel seeds,
lightly crushed
300ml/10fl oz/1¼ cups
chicken stock, warmed
1 onion, sliced
4 garlic cloves, sliced
4 fresh thyme sprigs
250ml/8fl oz/1 cup Guinness
2 tbsp clear honey

For the potato salad
900g/2lb small, waxy new
potatoes, scraped or scrubbed
2 tsp white wine vinegar
2 tbsp light olive oil
4-5 spring onions, trimmed
and thinly sliced
2 tbsp chopped fresh coriander
salt and pepper

METHOD

Preheat the oven to 350°F/180°C/ Gas Mark 4. Pour the cider and fennel seeds into a large jug with the chicken stock. Season lightly with salt and set aside. Place the onion in a roasting tray with the garlic and thyme. Place the rack of pork ribs on top of the vegetables in the roasting tray and add the cider and chicken stock. Cover with foil, and then bake for 1½-2 hours until the pork is tender and completely soft.

To make the Guinness reduction, pour the Guinness and honey into a pan and bring to the boil, then reduce the heat and allow to further reduce for 5–8 minutes until thickened.

When the pork ribs are cooked, brush with the Guinness reduction. Place in the oven for 15-30 minutes to enhance the flavour, continuously basting with the Guinness reduction.

To make the potato salad, cut the potatoes into 2.5cm/1-inch chunks. Place in a pan of salted water, bring to the boil and cook for 12-15 minutes or until tender. This will depend on your potatoes, so keep an eye on them in case they decide to be tricky. Meanwhile, whisk together the white wine vinegar and olive oil in a small bowl, season to taste.

Drain the potatoes well, transfer to a serving bowl and gently stir in the spring onion and chopped coriander.

SERVES 4-6

Lollipop Pork with a Honey, Apple & Cider Reduction

A fabulous pork dish that's a winner every time. Ask your local butcher to prepare the pork for you as I've described in the recipe. Their expertise will make your preparation so much easier.

INGREDIENTS

1kg/2lb 4oz or 4 rib bone
in loin of pork (bones
cleaned, and tied roast to
retain a round shape)
rock salt
6 shallots
250ml/9fl oz/1 cup cider
25g/1oz/2 tbsp butter
2 medium-sized cooking
apples, peeled and diced
2 tbsp honey
300ml/10fl oz/1¼ cups cider
½ tsp wholegrain mustard
1 tbsp cream or crème fraîche
salt and freshly ground
white pepper
chives, to garnish

Colcannon potatoes
675g/1lb 8oz potatoes,
well scrubbed
70g/2½oz/5 tbsp butter
6 tbsp cream

METHOD

Preheat the oven to 180°C/150°F/Gas Mark 4. Dry the pork thoroughly with kitchen towel, then season with some rock salt. Place the pork into a roasting tin. Cut the shallots in half lengthways and add them to the tray. Pour the dry cider into the baking tray.

Roast the pork for 30-45 minutes (allow an extra five minutes for every additional 250g/9oz of pork), checking occasionally that there's enough liquid in the roasting pan, topping up with a little hot water if needed. After 30-45 minutes, increase the temperature to 190°C/375°F/Gas Mark 5 to crisp the pork crackling. Cook the pork for another 25-35 minutes at this higher temperature (again allow an extra five minutes for every additional 250g/9oz of pork). Meanwhile, make the sauce and the colcannon potato. For the sauce, heat a medium-sized pot with the butter and add to it the peeled and diced cooking apples. Sauté them gently for 4-5 minutes and allow them to caramelise slightly. Next add in the honey and allow this to bubble up and melt down a little before adding in the cider and the wholegrain mustard. Allow this to boil and reduce for a few moments and then add in the cream or crème fraîche to enrich the sauce slightly. Continue to simmer for approximately 10-12 minutes and serve with the seared pork.

To make the Colcannon potatoes, place the potatoes in a pot and cover with water – just enough to cover them and no more. Bring to the boil, then simmer for 15-20 minutes or until completely tender when pierced with the tip of a sharp knife. Drain the potatoes in a colander and then peel while they are still hot. Push through a potato ricer or sieve using a spatula. Beat the butter into the warm mashed potato and then mix in the cream. Season to taste. Serve.

Roasted Leg of Lamb with Herb Crust

I just adore spring lamb, it has such a deliciously delicate flavour and this nice marmalade crust gives an unusual twist to the dish. All the Dundon family adore lamb and this recipe makes a delicious Sunday Roast for us to enjoy.

INGREDIENTS

1 leg of lamb
(approx 2kg/4lb 8oz)
3 carrots, peeled and cut
into large chunks
1 bulb of garlic, halved
horizontally
3 large onions,
roughly chopped
2-3 sprigs of rosemary
3 tbsp olive oil
salt and pepper

Wine and rosemary sauce
25g/1oz/2½ tbsp flour
½ tsp tomato purée
100ml/3½fl oz/scant
½ cup red wine
300ml/10fl oz/1¼ cups
good quality meat stock
½ tsp chopped rosemary

Mint sauce
200g/7oz fresh mint
leaves, finely chopped
2 tsp superfine sugar
60ml/2fl oz/generous
⅜ cup boiling water
125ml/4fl oz/½ cup white
wine vinegar

METHOD

Preheat the oven to 200°C/400°F/ Gas Mark 6. On a large roasting tray, arrange large chunks of the carrots, garlic and onion to form a trivet which will raise the meat off the bottom of the tray.

Lay the leg of lamb on top of the vegetables. Using a sharp knife make a number of incisions into the fat of the lamb and stick sprigs of the rosemary into them.

Season lightly with a little salt and pepper, drizzle with a little oil and roast in the oven for 1-1½ hours (15 minutes per 450g/1lb for rare and 20 minutes for medium), turning over halfway through.

Allow the meat to rest for at least 15 minutes before carving to allow the juices to soak into the flesh.

Wine and rosemary sauce
Drain the majority of the fat off the tray and put the tray on the stovetop. Sprinkle in the flour, add tomato purée and stir with a whisk until well coloured. Gradually pour in the red wine and stock and continue to whisk until the mixture comes to the boil. Sieve into a clean saucepan to remove any impurities.

Add the chopped rosemary and boil for 4-5 minutes until reduced and thickened nicely. Adjust the seasoning and pour into a sauce boat to accompany the lamb.

Mint sauce
Combine the mint and superfine sugar in a mixing bowl. Bring the water and vinegar to the boil. Pour over the mint and stir with a wooden spoon until the sugar dissolves.

Allow the sauce to stand for 15 minutes for the flavour to develop before serving in a sauce jug with a spoon.

Lamb Pasta Ragout

This pasta dish makes a hearty family meal. It works well with pasta but you can also try it with mashed potatoes or plain basmati rice.

INGREDIENTS

450g/1lb diced lamb
(neck or shoulder)
25g/1oz/2 tbsp butter
50ml/2fl oz/generous
3 tbsp brandy
2 sprigs of rosemary
bouquet garni
30ml/1fl oz/2 tbsp olive oil
2 large carrots, diced
1 large onion, diced
4 garlic cloves
55g/2oz/½ cup, firmly
packed plain flour
2 tbsp tomato purée
100ml/3½fl oz/scant
½ cup red wine
3 tbsp red wine vinegar
300ml/10fl oz/1¼ cups
lamb or beef stock
4 tbsp parsley, chopped
500-600g/1lb 2oz-1lb 5oz
penne pasta
200g/7oz cheddar or
Parmesan cheese

METHOD

Preheat the oven to 180°C/350°F/ Gas Mark 4. Trim any excess fat or sinew off the lamb.

Heat a large heavy-based frying pan with a little butter and, in batches, brown off the diced lamb. Return the lamb to the pan, then flambé it with the brandy, taking care, as ever, to move any flammable materials out of the way and to switch your extractor fan off. Transfer to a large casserole dish and add the sprigs of rosemary and bouquet garni.

Drizzle a little olive oil into the same pan you used for the lamb, then add the carrots, onions and diced garlic, and cook these for a few minutes over a medium heat until the vegetables have slightly caramelised. Sprinkle the flour over the vegetables and add the tomato purée. Season with some salt and freshly ground black pepper.

Pour in the red wine, red wine vinegar and beef stock at this stage. Allow the entire mixture to come to the boil.

Pour this over the lamb in the casserole dish (which already has the bouquet garni and fresh rosemary tucked safely in there) and cover the casserole.

Transfer to the oven for up to 2 hours until the meat is nice and tender, then remove the bouquet garni and rosemary sprigs and discard. Pour the casserole contents into the base of a large ovenproof dish.

Thirty minutes before serving, cook the pasta as per pack instructions. Serve the ragout on top of the pasta, with shavings of cheese sprinkled over the ragout and get stuck in, immediately.

Roast Rack of Lamb with Pea Purée

Spring lamb is absolutely delicious. Spring lamb is the meat from milk-fed lamb that is between three and five months old. It tends to be more tender and not to have that strong lamb taste and scent which is synonymous with older lambs. In this particular recipe, I have chosen to serve it with a delicious pea purée, which has a wonderfully delicate colour.

INGREDIENTS

4 individual portions
of rack of lamb
(approximately 3 bones each)
4 English mustard
freshly chopped parsley
1 tbsp plain flour
100ml/3½fl oz/scant
½ cup of red wine
250ml/8fl oz/1 cup beef
or lamb stock, warmed
1 tsp tomato purée
fresh rosemary
fresh thyme

Pea purée
1 tbsp olive oil
½ medium-sized onion
2 garlic cloves
225g/8oz frozen peas
200ml/7fl oz/generous
¾ cup cream
salt and pepper

METHOD

Spread the mustard on the racks of lamb. Mix the parsley and press onto the crust of the lamb racks. Bake in a hot oven for 20-25 minutes depending on how you like you meat cooked. Allow to rest in the oven for 5 minutes. Carve as required.

In the meantime, in a large saucepan quickly fry off the onion and garlic until lightly browned. Add in the frozen peas and coat them with onion and garlic mixture. Add in the cream and cook until the peas have softened and the cream has reduced and thickened which will take about 5 minutes. Mix in the seasoning at this stage.

Transfer the entire mixture to a food processor or use a handheld blitzer and blend until completely smooth.

When the lamb is baked, take it out of the oven and leave aside to rest. Remove the grease from the roasting tin and place the tin on direct heat. Scatter in the flour, then pour in the red wine and beef stock with a little tomato purée.

Bring to the boil. Add some chopped rosemary or thyme. Sieve the mixture into a clean saucepan and boil to reduce. Serve as required.

SERVES 4

Braised Lamb Shanks with Garlic Mash

Turn your plain old mash into glorious garlic mash to accompany this melt in the mouth lamb dish. Make it once, and your guests will always demand this dish from you!

INGREDIENTS

4 lamb shanks
115g/4oz/1 cup,
firmly packed plain flour
with the addition of
Salt and Pepper
18 pearl onions
3 carrots, peeled and
diced into chunks
1 level tsp tomato purée
300ml/10fl oz/1¼ cups
red wine
425ml/15fl oz/generous 1¾
cups chicken or lamb stock
1 bunch of thyme
1 bay leaf
2–3 sprigs of rosemary
4 garlic cloves
salt and pepper

The potatoes
8 rooster potatoes
1 bulb garlic
1 tsp sunflower oil
115g/4oz/½ cup butter
pinch of salt

METHOD

Cut the vegetables into large chunks, then coat the lamb shanks in the seasoned flour.

Heat a large deep pan and seal the lamb shanks. Remove from the pan and transfer to a large casserole dish.

Add the remainder of the seasoned flour left over after coating the lamb to the pan and stir around until it has darkened in colour and soaked up all the residue from the pan. Stir in the tomato purée.

Pour the wine and stock into the pan, bring to the boil and reduce by about a third. Put the vegetables into the casserole pot with the lamb, together with the herbs and seasoning. Add the reduced wine and the stock to the casserole dish and cover.

Bake in the oven for 2-2½ hours at 160°C/325°F/Gas Mark 3.

Remove from the oven and make sure the meat is tender; if not, return to the oven for another few minutes.

Remove the meat from the casserole dish and boil the liquid until reduced or thickened.

Wrap the garlic bulb in tin foil with the sunflower oil and roast in the oven alongside the lamb shanks for approximately 45 minutes. Meanwhile peel the potatoes and put them into a large saucepan and cover with water, bring to the boil and boil until tender.

Strain off the water and leave to steam in the saucepan for 5–6 minutes to continue to soften. Remove the garlic bulb from the oven and squeeze out the garlic pulp. Mash the potatoes with the butter and add the garlic pulp, mix well and season as required. Return the lamb to the sauce and serve alongside the potatoes. Garnish with freshly chopped parsley.

SERVES 4-6

Beef & Irish Stout Stew

The stout not only tenderises the beef but also adds a lovely malty dimension to the stew.

INGREDIENTS

675g/1lb 8oz lean beef, cut into 2cm/1-inch cubes
2 tbsp olive oil
25g/1oz/2 tbsp butter
2 large onions, sliced
2 garlic cloves
150g/5½oz carrots
150g/5½oz celery
150g/5½oz parsnip
2 sprigs thyme
25g/1oz/¼ cup plain flour
2 tsp tomato purée
500ml/17fl oz/generous 2 cups Irish stout
300ml/10fl oz/1¼ cups beef stock, warmed
2 tsp Worcestershire sauce
salt and pepper, to season

METHOD

Drizzle some olive oil into a pan over a medium heat and add a knob of butter. Add the meat to the pan in batches and quickly brown. Remove the meat from the pan and place in a casserole dish, season lightly.

Using the same pan, add the remaining butter, then add the onion, garlic, carrots, celery, parsnip and thyme and cook for 3–5 minutes. Season well.

Sprinkle the flour over the vegetables, then add the tomato purée, cook for a further 4-5 minutes. Pour in the stout and warmed beef stock and few drops of Worcestershire sauce.

Pour the pan contents into the casserole dish, cover with a tight-fitting lid and place in a preheated oven at 150°C/300°F/ Gas Mark 2 for 2-3 hours, checking occasionally to ensure there is enough liquid in the dish.

Once cooked, remove from the oven and check the consistency of the cooking juice. If too thick, add a little extra beef stock; if too thin, let it reduce down for a few minutes extra until you've got a nice gravy-like consistency.

Serve immediately on its own or with some mashed potatoes to soak up the liquid.

FROM SLAVE TO SAINT: THE REAL STORY OF ST. PATRICK

Consider St. Patrick's Day. It's a public celebration of Irishness everywhere. Observed every 17th of March, it not only commemorates the patron saint of Ireland, it also acknowledges the impact of Irish people across the world. Who could be more Irish than St. Patrick himself – the man who single-handedly brought Christianity to Ireland by converting the pagan High King Laoghaire on Easter Day? The saint who famously banished the snakes from Irish shores!

Well it can come as a shock to most people to learn that Patrick wasn't actually Irish. He wasn't born in Ireland. And he didn't set foot on the Emerald Isle until he was nearly 16 years old. What's the real story?

Patrick, scholars say, was born in a village in Britain that was occupied by Romans. His father was a deacon from a Roman family, his mother a relative of the patron St. Martin of Tours. The one thing they certainly weren't was Irish. Surprising, isn't it?

Later writers created a bit of a St. Patrick cult, spreading the myth that it was Patrick who first brought Christianity to Ireland where it quickly replaced the established pagan deities. In fact, a man called Palladius was sent from Rome to Ireland in 431 to become the first bishop of Ireland. Palladius already had been successful as a missionary long before Patrick began his own mission.

No snakes please, he's British!

Patrick's first experience in Ireland was a brutal one. At the age of 15 or 16, he was captured by Irish pirates and sold into slavery. He then spent six years as a shepherd in what may have been County Mayo where he began to pray hard every day. His prayers were answered six years later, not by the overnight conversion of Ireland to Christianity but by an opportunity to escape and sail back to his family. He just wanted to get home.

It was only after he was safely in Britain that Patrick decided his mission in life was to return to Ireland as a Christian evangelist. Those snakes? Unfortunately, the long cherished story of St. Patrick's banishing the snakes from Ireland is just another myth. There were no snakes in Ireland to expel. However, Patrick did do more than anyone at the time to spread Christianity in Ireland so that the church was well established by the time of his death. As with many so-called "truths" about Ireland, the St. Patrick legend owes as much to brilliant storytelling as it does to cold, hard facts.

"This is one race of people for whom psychoanalysis is of no use whatsoever."

Sigmund Freud (about the Irish)

SERVES 4-6

Braised Beef Cheeks

Braising is such a wonderful method of cooking the tougher cuts of meat. The result is melt-in-your-mouth beef with oodles of flavour.

INGREDIENTS

900g/2lb beef cheeks,
cut into chunks
20g/¾oz/scant 2 tbsp butter
1 tbsp olive oil
4 small carrots cut in
half lengthways
2 large onions, diced
4-8 baby leeks, thinly sliced
4 garlic cloves chopped
1 tsp fresh herbs
(rosemary and thyme)
55g/2oz/½ cup, firmly
packed plain flour
2 tsp cracked black peppercorns
3 tbsp brandy
850ml/1½ pints/
3¾ cups beef stock
200ml/7fl oz/generous
¾ cup red wine
1 tsp tomato purée
chopped parsley, to garnish

METHOD

Preheat the oven to 150°C/300°F/ Gas Mark 2. Melt the butter in a large pan with a splash of oil and quickly brown off the meat in batches until it is browned all over. Make sure not to place too much meat in the saucepan at any given time because the meat will begin to stew. Transfer the meat to a large casserole dish.

Add the sliced carrots, onion, leeks, and garlic to the pot that you cooked the meat in. Add a sprig or two of rosemary and thyme. Scatter in the plain flour and the crushed black peppercorns over the vegetables and herbs and mix well over a low heat.

Pour in the brandy and flambée the alcohol taking care to ensure you move anything flammable well out of the way. Then, whoosh!

Add the beef stock and red wine, stirring gently with a wooden spoon to combine the flour with the liquid and to lightly thicken the sauce. Bring the sauce to the boil for 4-5 minutes. Stir in the tomato purée and then taste the sauce, correcting the seasoning if you feel some more salt or pepper is needed.

Pour the contents of the pot into the casserole dish over the meat and cover with a tight-fitting lid. Transfer to the oven for approximately 3-3½ hours. Don't forget to take the dish out of the oven every so often (perhaps every 50 minutes to 1 hour) to give it a good old stir and to make sure that the liquid has not evaporated off. Add a little more beef stock if necessary.

Serve with some baby boiled potatoes dressed with butter and chopped parsley or with a large chunk of bread and a glass of a good full-bodied merlot wine.

SERVES 4

Beef Curry Pie

Steak AND curry, two of my favourite foods in a pie! It doesn't get better than this for us steak and curry lovers. This is the perfect way to serve up a quick, tasty, family supper.

INGREDIENTS

600g/1lb 8oz sirloin beef, cut into thin strips
2 tbsp olive oil
1 medium sized onion, sliced very thinly
3 garlic cloves, diced
½ red chilli, finely diced
3 carrots, sliced
1 leek, chopped
½ tsp turmeric
1 tsp tomato purée
2 tsp red curry paste
200ml/7fl oz/generous ¾ cup red wine
600ml/1 pint/2½ cups beef stock, boiling hot
salt and pepper
4 sheets puff pastry
1 egg yolk beaten with 2 tsp water, for egg wash

METHOD

Drizzle some oil into a saucepan over a high heat and add the beef strips. Cook for 4-5 minutes stirring occasionally until the beef is sealed (browned) all over, then season lightly with a little salt and pepper.

Next add in the sliced onions, garlic, chilli, carrots, leeks and turmeric. Allow them to cook quite gently until they are softened and glazed with the meat juices for about 4-5 minutes.

Squeeze in the tomato purée and curry paste and allow this mixture to coat the meat. This will give the curry a developed taste and flavour as well as helping with the formation of good colour.

Pour over the red wine and deglaze the pan, stirring the bottom to catch any remnants lingering there. Next pour in the hot beef stock and allow this mixture to come to the boil. Reduce the heat and allow to simmer gently, covered with a lid, for another 40-50 minutes.

Grease a large pie dish and dust it with flour before lining it with the puff pastry. Keep some pastry aside to be used as the lid.

Fill the pastry-lined pie dish with the meat and brush the edges with the egg wash. Pop the top on the pie, then brush with the egg wash and pierce the centre.

Bake in a preheated oven at 200°C/400°F/Gas Mark 6 for 20-25 minutes until the pastry is crisp and golden.

Remove from the oven and serve immediately with apple chutney and watercress leaves.

SERVES 8

Kevin's Homemade Burgers with Red Onion Marmalade

You can cook the burgers at the barbecue or transfer the burgers to a baking sheet and put them into a preheated oven for 8-10 minutes until they are fully cooked.

INGREDIENTS

675g/1lb 8oz lean minced beef
2 spring onions
2 garlic cloves
55g/2oz breadcrumbs
55g/2oz/¼ cup
Parmesan, grated
2-4 tsp parsley and thyme,
freshly chopped
2 tsp tomato ketchup or
sweet chilli jam (optional)
pinch cinnamon
1 large egg
2 tbsp olive oil
4-6 slices mature
cheddar cheese
6 slices streaky bacon, grilled
2 tomatoes
salt and pepper

mixed salad leaves, to serve

Red onion marmalade
4 red onions
55g/2oz/¼ cup, firmly
packed brown sugar
50ml/1¾fl oz/scant
¼ cup red wine
50ml/1¾fl oz/scant
¼ cup red wine vinegar

METHOD

Preheat the barbecue. Put the minced beef into a large mixing bowl and add the finely diced onions and garlic. Mix in the breadcrumbs, grated cheese and chopped parsley together with the tomato ketchup and add a pinch of cinnamon. Season the mixture with a little salt and pepper. Add in the egg and mash the mixture together with your hands using the egg as a binding agent.

Divide the mixture into 8-9 pieces and using a little plain flour shape them into your desired shapes about 1cm/½ inch thick. Allow to rest in the fridge for at least 30 minutes.

Drizzle some oil in a griddle pan. When hot, add the burgers 4 at a time. Cook for 4-5 minutes each side depending on thickness.

In the meantime drizzle the halved buns with olive oil and reheat on barbecue. Immediately add the burgers and cheese slices, then build your own burger adding the tomatoes, streaky bacon and mixed salad leaves as required.

Red onion marmalade
Thinly slice the red onions and sauté off over a moderate heat. When they're nicely browned, add in some brown sugar and allow to caramelise.

Add red wine and red wine vinegar and allow to cook out to a sticky consistency. Serve with the burgers.

Oven Baked Joint Rib of Beef with Baked Potatoes & Béarnaise Sauce

The flavour of the beef cooked on the bone is far superior to when it is cooked off it. You can serve it with baby potatoes or baked potatoes.

INGREDIENTS

2 ribs of beef (on the bone)
approximately 450g/1lb each
20 baby potatoes
200g/7oz parsnip,
cut into large chunks
2 tbsp olive oil
1 sprig of rosemary
400g/14oz pearl onions
50g/1¾oz/3 generous
tbsp butter
10g/⅓ oz/scant 1 tbsp sugar
1 large onion, chopped
2 carrots, chopped
salt and pepper

Béarnaise sauce
1 small shallot, very
finely diced
½ tsp white wine vinegar
3 egg yolks
100g/3½oz/scant ½ cup butter,
melted and cooled
1 tsp chopped fresh tarragon

METHOD

Preheat the oven to 200°C/400°F/ Gas Mark 6. Place the baby potatoes in a large pan, cover with salted water and bring to the boil for 15–20 minutes until tender, drain and set aside.

Place the parsnip chunks on a baking tray, drizzle with some olive oil and place in the oven for 20 minutes, until softened.

In a sauté pan, add the pearl onions and pour in one glass of water, half the butter, the sugar and seasoning. Bring to the boil, and simmer for 5–10 minutes until the water has evaporated and the onions are slightly caramelised.

Select a large frying pan and heat it with a little oil. Sear the rib of beef in the pan at high heat, and then transfer to the oven on a tray with the roughly chopped onion and carrots as a bed for the ribs. Bake for 20-25 minutes for medium and over 30 minutes for well done.

Béarnaise sauce
Have a pot of water simmering away on the cooker.

In a bowl, infuse the chopped shallot with the white wine vinegar and place over the heat in a separate pan for a minute or two. Add the egg yolks and whisk continuously until the colour lightens and the mixture thickens. It should take about 5 minutes or so.

You need to keep whisking the mixture. Taking it on and off the heat as required to prevent it scrambling.

Slowly add in the melted butter, whisking continuously at all times. Taste the sauce, correct the seasoning if necessary and add in some freshly chopped tarragon to taste. Serve immediately with the beef and baby potatoes.

INGREDIENTS
Baked potatoes
675g/1lb 8oz floury potatoes
such as Rooster or Golden
Wonder, cut into large
even-sized chunks
vegetable oil or dripping,
goose or duck fat
Maldon sea salt

METHOD
This dish can also be served
with baked potatoes.

Preheat the oven to 220°C/425°F/
Gas Mark 7. Place the potatoes
in a pan of cold salted water
and bring to the boil. Reduce the
heat, cover and simmer for
8-10 minutes until the outsides
have just softened. Drain and
return to the pan for a minute
or two to dry out.

Meanwhile, preheat a roasting
tin with 1cm/½ inch of oil,
dripping, duck or goose fat for a
few minutes until just smoking.
Put the lid back on the potatoes

and shake vigorously to break up
and soften the edges or roughly
prod the outside of the potatoes
with a fork. Carefully tip them
into the hot oil, basting the tops.

Place the roasting tin with
the potatoes back in the oven
and cook for 40 minutes, then
pour off the majority of the fat
before turning the potatoes over.
Season to taste with the salt and
cook for a further 20 minutes
until crispy around the edges
and golden brown.

To serve, tip the roast potatoes
into a warmed serving dish.

Kevin's tip
The beef should be aged for at least twenty-one days. Look for good
marbling of fat, which will ensure a succulent joint when roasting.

Roast the beef at a high temperature for about 15 minutes to get the
heat through to the centre of the joint. Then reduce the temperature
to 160°C/325°F/Gas Mark 3 and continue to roast for 12-13 minutes
per 450g/1lb for rare, 17-18 minutes per 450g/1lb for medium, or
22-24 minutes per 450g/1lb for well done.

Ensure you allow the beef to rest for as long as possible before
carving. This allows the meat fibres – which contract in the oven –
to relax again, so the meat will be tenderer.

SERVES 4

Striploin of Beef with Marmalade Butter & Pomme Pont-neuf

Naturally succulent and delicious, striploin has always been the most popular cut for steaks. It's relatively lean, very versatile, easy to prepare and perfect to pan fry, grill or barbeque.

INGREDIENTS

4 striploin steaks,
200-225g/7-8oz each
sprigs of thyme and rosemary
2 bay leaves
3-4 black peppercorns
75ml/2½fl oz/5 tbsp olive oil

Marmalade butter
100g/3½oz/scant ½ cup butter
1 tbsp orange marmalade

Pommes Pont-neuf
potatoes (Maris Piper
or similar)
salt and pepper

METHOD

Place the thyme, rosemary and bay leaves into a large bowl with the black peppercorns. Pour in the oil and mix thoroughly to allow the flavours to infuse. Place the striploin steaks into the marinade and leave them to marinade for up to 2 hours or preferably overnight.

Then in a small bowl, soften some butter with a spatula and add in a spoonful of marmalade, combine until smooth. Store in the fridge until required.

Preheat the deepfat fryer to 160°C/325°F, peel the potatoes and cut them into chip-size batons (1cm/½ inch thick), then place in a bowl filled with water to store until required.

When required, place these pommes pont-neuf on a clean kitchen towel, and pat dry to get rid of any excess of water. Place them into the first oil. Deep fry for 3-5 minutes without coloration. This step helps the pommes pont-neuf to become fluffy and cook thoroughly. Remove from the oil and increase the temperature to 190°C/375°F. When the oil is ready, place the pommes pont-neuf back in the oil and deep fry another 4-5 minutes until crisp and golden.

Remove from the oil and place in a bowl lined with kitchen paper to absorb excess oil.

Meanwhile, preheat a ridged griddle pan over a medium-high heat. Brush the steaks with 1 tablespoon olive oil and season to taste with salt and pepper. Sear the steaks for 2-3 minutes each side (for a medium finish), or longer if desired.

Divide the pommes pont-neuf between 4 plates, then place a steak on top. Add a spoonful of the marmalade butter and allow to melt over the steak. Season and serve immediately.

HUGHES'S PUB, THE FOUR COURTS, DUBLIN, IRELAND.

John Cooke: Multi-tasker

It is 8 a.m. at Hughes's pub in the markets area of Dublin, and the pub is buzzing with activity. The markets district in Dublin sits next door to the Four Courts, Ireland's main court buildings. Hughes's is where Ireland's legal centre and teeming markets meet at a crossroads. Market traders drink hot whiskeys and banter loudly in one corner while barristers in wigs and gowns whisper to clients who will appear before a judge later that morning. Our journey to Raglan Road brings us to a table where a young John Cooke sits with his father. He was awake at 5 a.m. and already has spent several hours buying fish with this father in the Corporation Fish Market.

"It was common then for all the family to work in the family business, and it's where my interest and passion for food began," Cooke recalls. "I was fascinated by the smells and noises of the bustling markets, the massive canyons of stacked boxes of fresh-caught fish, the fruit and vegetable stands that seemed to go on for miles."

In an hour's time, young John will be dropped off at school. After school, he will work behind the counter in the family fish and poultry shop in Stillorgan.

"In those days, almost every fish caught off Ireland came into Dublin and was auctioned off at the Corporation Market beside the Four Courts," John explains. "Fish might be caught down in Wexford, brought up to Dublin, auctioned in the morning, bought, filleted at Cooke's shop, then packed, put on a train back to Wexford for one of our customers the same afternoon."

Some mornings after visiting the fish market, John and his father would stop in at Hughes's pub, one of the early houses that opened at 5 a.m. "It was kind of an interesting place," he says, with great understatement.

Fish ran or, rather, swam in the Cooke family. John's grandfather owned and ran a fish-and-chip shop called George's Café at 46 South Richmond Street in Dublin. The family, including John's father, Les, and four siblings lived above the cafe. During the Second World War, or "The Emergency" as it was known in Ireland, coal was hard to come by. Les and his siblings would travel into the Dublin Mountains to cut turf and then bring it back to the shop for fuel to keep the range going to cook the fish and chips.

In the late 1950s, John's grandfather moved the family to Stillorgan in south Dublin and entered the fish and poultry business. John, the eldest of six children, recalls the frenzy of preparing for holiday turkey sales.

"At Christmas, we used to sell thousands of turkeys to housewives," he says. "I would pack the giblets into little bags to make sure each housewife got what she needed to make her gravy."

John's affection for the family business continued into his college years when he worked nearly full-time even during exams. His fond memories of a very close extended family are vivid. "There were always parties and big Sunday lunches after church with 20 or 30 people at my grandparents' house," John remembers.

When John's father, Les Cooke, wasn't running the shop, he was performing as a big band singer. Les had a residency at The Shelbourne Hotel with the Noel Kelehan Quartet. He would sing at The Shelbourne in the evening, go home to take a shower, then go out to work at the fish markets in the early hours of the morning. He earned a gold record for the song "The Donegal Waltz," sang in the fourth Irish National Song Contest in 1968 and did the first-ever light-entertainment live outdoor broadcast for the Irish national TV broadcaster RTE (Raidio Teilifis Eireann). Even while pursuing his career in entertainment, he put in the hours at the fish and poultry business during the day. John's mother, Kay, also worked in the business – behind the counter of the shop during the day and doing the books on the kitchen table at night. "Work was certainly something I was very aware of growing up," John says. "We all worked – Mom, Dad, my siblings."

Les Cooke entered the pub and restaurant business in County Dublin in the 1970s. "I was pulling pints in the bar from the time I was 15," John fondly recalls. "You'd open at 10:30 a.m., then you'd have the 'Holy Hour' at 2:30 to 3:30 p.m. each day when you had to close, then you'd reopen after that." The business of being a publican was viewed as a true trade and profession back then, with apprenticeships to be served and long hours worked. There was no such thing as a work-life balance.

Les, a man of extraordinary energy, character and enterprise, is in the Guinness Book of World Records for buying the dearest strawberries at a 1977 charity auction for a record £530 Irish punt (equivalent to the British pound) to generate publicity for his business.

Like father, like son. John knew his career would follow a similar path.

"Some people say I have an innate sense of hospitality – I think I can thank the large family gatherings that were a constant while I was growing up," he says.

John's first opportunity to work at something very different from the fish or the pub business – location-based, multi-dimensional entertainment – came in the late 1980s.

"This was a fun and interesting time," John says, recalling that much of what this new job involved was creating environments where people could have fun, including everything from Ten Pin Bowling and Lazer Tag to Virtual Reality simulators. John travelled a lot during this time through Europe, North and South America and across Asia.

"What was most enlightening about travelling was that it gave me a much stronger sense of what it means to be Irish – a greater sense and appreciation of Irish culture and so on," John says. "I believe Bono once said something like 'in order to truly understand about what being Irish is, you need to go away to be able to look back.'" John didn't realize it at the time, but gaining this perspective would later play an important part on the Road to Raglan.

John's career led him to work with a Dublin-based hospitality design and consulting company, where he continued his travels while working on projects that included casinos in Australia, nationally branded pub chains in the United Kingdom, landmark hotel projects in the United Arab Emirates and casinos in Las Vegas.

"These projects were very enjoyable," John says. "Coming from a relatively small country like Ireland and finding yourself standing in the middle of a huge landmark project in a world-famous location and to be part of it, well, it just gave you a buzz."

John views this part of his career as key to the Raglan Road story. The venues and projects he worked on were large, had scale, and certainly influenced and shaped Raglan Road. The company also operated the Irish Pub Company, which designed and built hundreds of authentic Irish pubs all over the world.

"I was involved in many of them and, what struck me was that, when done well, these pubs were great," John says. "I remember sitting at the bar on opening night at P.J. O'Brien's in Melbourne, Australia and thinking, 'this is really good, I mean really good, the atmosphere, the hospitality, it feels like home and yet we are thousands of miles away.'"

It was also during this part of the journey to Raglan Road that John met Paul Nolan, who was group marketing director at the company. "Between that gig and Raglan Road, Paul and I have been working together for over 15 years – that must be an anniversary of some sort," John says, laughing. "Never even sent me a card!"

When Paul and John travelled the world working on hospitality projects, Irish Pub included, they noticed that many types of concepts had developed into larger-scale venues. But so far, the Irish Pub had not.

"Paul and I used to speculate that, if you built a really brilliant Irish Pub of scale with the best that Irish craftspeople could produce, creating real contemporary Irish food, bringing authentic talent and entertainment from Ireland, and you ran it with a true sense of Irish hospitality, you could rival the best of the best in the industry," he says.

The opportunity to create a larger, more authentic pub came in 2001-'02, when the Irish Pub Company was selected by MGM to create a flagship Irish pub. Nine Fine Irishmen opened at New York New York on the Las Vegas Strip in 2003. The pub, developed, opened and managed by John and Paul, created a stir from the get-go and quickly became the top account in the United States for a certain well know Irish Beer. "Nine Fine Irishmen had many firsts. I think that the approach to food, though, was the biggest change for Irish pubs in North America," John says. "Kevin Dundon's food, or anything like it, had never been seen inside the door of an Irish Pub in North America. Oh, and did I mention that Nine Fine Irishmen was when we first started to work with Kevin, the third musketeer, 10 years this year it is, another guy who owes me a card."

Nine Fine Irishmen helped to redefine expectations around Irish pubs in America. Disney officials, curious about reports of its popularity, traveled to Las Vegas to see it.

"Disney's own research in Orlando was telling them that people wanted to see an Irish pub there," he says. "Christmas came a little early 2004, December 24th to be exact, which is when the contract with Disney to open Raglan Road was signed."

In creating Raglan Road, John, Paul and Kevin had the opportunity to again raise the bar for authentic Irish Pub Restaurants.

"Raglan Road would significantly exceed Las Vegas in terms of size, which was a challenge we all relished," John recounted. Even greater scale would allow the partners to do things in Orlando that could not be achieved in Las Vegas. "In many respects, we wanted to create an even purer pub, a real Dublin Pub. Raglan would look and feel like a Dublin Victorian pub that had been lifted off the streets of Dublin and placed in the middle of Walt Disney World."

The greatest compliments are paid by your guests and especially by guests who know. Not long after opening, John met a customer at the bar in Raglan Road. "With a little sadness, he said that he had emigrated to the United States over 30 years ago and had not been home since," John says. "Walking into Raglan Road was, he said, 'like walking into any pub on Baggot Street.'" Well, it seems Raglan Road got that one right.

"Being here in this wonderful place, I am very fortunate. I get to work with great like-minded people, Paul, Kevin, and our fantastic management led by Sean and Lorraine," John says. "It is a privileged existence. Raglan Road allows me to exercise my passion for food and hospitality, showcase my culture and indulge my interest in music and entertainment." The food – and the respect, appreciation and enjoyment of it – as well as the entertainment, have been, in one way or another, part of the Cooke family business for generations.

It is a long way from the markets of Dublin and George's Café on South Richmond Street, but it's fairly certain that John's father and grandfather would approve of Raglan Road in their own very modest Irish way.

"I think they would," John says, "although being a lot like me, they were always a little restless, seeking to improve, innovate and do things better. I suspect they might have a helpful suggestion or two!"

Chicken

Who doesn't like chicken? It's light, it's quick and simple to prepare and cook, and it has to be one of the most versatile meats to include in a recipe. It works well in classics like my Homemade Chicken Kiev or my simple roast Stuffed Chicken with Roasted Root Vegetables, but it's equally well suited to pies like my Creamy Forest Mushroom & Free Range Chicken Pie. Chicken also is perfect in spicy curry dishes like my Thai Coconut Chicken Curry with Pilau Rice and salads like my Taste of the Orient Grilled Chicken Salad. All in all, the humble chicken is one succulent and super-adaptable bird. These recipes won't have you clucking over lots of tricky preparation, they're simple and straightforward, so get cooking!

SERVES 4

Taste of the Orient Grilled Chicken Salad

People tell me that they are looking for new ways of jazzing up chicken. Well, this marinade adds a subtle taste of Asia to spice up your day without overpowering the chicken.

INGREDIENTS

4 chicken fillets, split open or butterflied
500g/1lb 2oz mixed green leaves such as arugula
1 lemon, juiced
3 tbsp olive oil
50g/1¾ oz/4 tbsp sesame seeds

Marinade
1 tbsp green curry paste
2 tbsp fish sauce
2 tbsp sunflower oil
salt and pepper

METHOD

Place the curry paste and fish sauce in a bowl and drizzle in the sunflower oil. Season with some salt and pepper. Prepare the chicken by making some incisions in the fillets to allow the marinade to permeate them.

With a small palette knife, spread the paste over the chicken fillets until all of the chicken has been fully coated, then place them into a shallow dish and leave to marinate for about two hours.

Preheat a griddle pan on high heat. Grill the chicken on both sides, keeping the heat on a medium strength for 5-6 minutes on each side ensuring that it is well cooked through to the centre.

Place the mixed leaves in a bowl, drizzle in the lemon juice and olive oil, stir in. Arrange a piece of chicken on top of each portion of salad and sprinkle with toasted sesame seeds.

Serve with some fresh salad greens or noodles.

SERVES 4

Homemade Chicken Kiev

Chicken Kiev is easy to prepare, stylish and a very tasty dish that you can serve on special occasions or just enjoy any time.

INGREDIENTS

4 large chicken fillets
4 garlic cloves
115g/4oz/½ cup butter
1 tbsp parsley, finely chopped
2 eggs
50ml/scant ¼ cup/
1¾fl oz milk
plain flour, seasoned
with salt and pepper
fresh white breadcrumbs,
approx. 175g/6oz/3 cups
salt and pepper

METHOD

Begin by making the garlic butter. Finely dice the garlic and add it to the softened butter with some freshly chopped parsley and some seasoning. Mix this together until thoroughly combined. You can store it like this until required or alternatively you can mould it between a piece of parchment paper and freeze it in a cylindrical shape. It's handy to have to hand in the freezer to liven up a piece of meat or to mix into some hot pasta.

With a sharp knife, create a pocket in the side of the chicken opening it out like a book. Divide the garlic butter between the four chicken breasts and close over the flap again to make sure that the garlic butter is encased inside the chicken.

Preheat the oven to 180°C/350°F/ Gas Mark 4.

Beat the eggs together with the milk. Dip the chicken into the seasoned flour, and make sure it is well coated. Shake off the excess and then dip the floured chicken into the 'eggy' mixture. It is important that the chicken is coated entirely with this mixture, which acts as the 'glue' so it can be completely coated with the breadcrumbs.

Dip the chicken in the fresh white breadcrumbs and gently press them onto the chicken until it's well coated.

Pan-fry the chicken on both sides over a moderate heat until it is golden brown. Transfer to a flat baking sheet and pop into the oven for an additional 20-22 minutes until the chicken is well cooked through.

Serve with a large green salad and some baby boiled potatoes.

SERVES 4

Oven Baked Poussin with Sage & Roasted Garlic

Poussins are the smallest chickens available to buy. I love them. Not just because they are very tender and quick to cook but also because each one is a perfect portion size, making them great to serve at dinner parties.

INGREDIENTS

4 oven-ready poussins
12 spring onions, trimmed
2 tbsp olive oil
85g/3oz/generous ⅓ cup butter, at room temperature
8 fresh sage leaves, plus extra to garnish
2 garlic cloves, thinly sliced
225g/8oz Swiss chard, thick stalks removed and roughly chopped
coarse sea salt and freshly ground black pepper

METHOD

Preheat the oven to 180°C/150°F/ Gas Mark 4. Arrange the spring onions in a roasting tin. Season generously and toss in half the olive oil until the onions are evenly coated.

Loosen the skin around the neck of each poussin and push a little of the butter under the skin until evenly spread over the breast, then push a sage leaf down each side so that they are clearly visible.

Arrange the poussins on the bed of spring onions and scatter the garlic over them. Drizzle over the remaining olive oil and season to taste. Roast for 35 minutes until the poussins are completely tender and golden brown. Leave to rest in a warm place for at least 10 minutes.

To serve, heat the remaining knob of butter in a pan and quickly sauté the chard for a minute or two until wilted. Season to taste and divide among warmed serving plates. Add some of the roasted spring onions to each one and sit a poussin on top. Scatter over the sage leaves to garnish.

"I showed my appreciation
of my native land in
the usual Irish way:
by getting out of it as soon
as I possibly could."

George Bernard Shaw (Irish playwright)

NO TIME LIKE THE PRESENT

The first mechanical public clock in Ireland was erected in 1466 at a medieval toll booth or "tholsel" near Christ Church in Dublin. Unlike modern clocks, it didn't have a face and marked only the hours of the day by striking a bell. Although Dubliners could work out the time from the clock, the time it told was local Dublin time. There was no single national time applied across Ireland until more than 400 years later, in 1880.

Before then, towns calculated the time locally by using the sun's meridian—the position of the sun at midday—which meant that every town had, in effect, its own time zone. This wasn't a big problem in an age when travel between towns in Ireland was rare and slow, and portable timepieces were few. Travelers simply adjusted to the time when they arrived in a new town without realizing that they had traveled in time as well as space. Cork time, for instance, was 11 minutes behind Dublin time until the late 1800s.

Back then, most people measured time by reference to sunrise, midday and sunset during the day. At night, time was noted by the position of the stars. The Irish took seasonal variations in stride. A day was a day—sunrise to sunset—whether it lasted 17 hours mid-summer or just eight hours in the depths of winter.

Railway time v. Local time

By 1880, as railways sped up travel throughout Ireland, there was a need for one national time. The Definition of Time Act was passed, creating mean time for Ireland at Dunsink Observatory in Castleknock, Dublin. Dunsink Mean Time (the average of all times in Ireland) was set at 25 minutes and 21 seconds behind Greenwich Mean Time in London. As a result, railways often had two clocks. One showed the old local time; the other presented the new Railway or Dublin time.

Gradually, Dunsink Mean Time took over and remained until 1916, the year of the Easter Rising, when Ireland adopted Greenwich Mean Time (GMT) for the duration of the First World War, bringing it in line with Britain. In 1923, following the war of independence, the new republic debated whether to stick with GMT or go back to Dunsink Mean Time and decided to keep GMT despite calls to restore "Dublin time." If the vote had gone the other way, time in Dublin today would be almost half an hour behind Belfast.

SERVES 4

Stuffed Chicken with Roasted Root Vegetables

Roast chicken is a family favourite and, of course, it makes the perfect Sunday lunch. But try adding some lemon or garlic to the basting butter for the most wonderful aromas and flavours.

INGREDIENTS

1 large chicken
115g/4oz butter/½ cup
½ medium-sized onion, diced
grated zest of 1 lemon
2 tbsp freshly chopped sage/
parsley/thyme/rosemary
225g/8oz/4 cups soft
white breadcrumbs
½ lemon
salt and pepper

Roasted root vegetables
8 small carrots,
halved lengthways
4 small parsnips, halved
12 large shallots,
peeled and trimmed
1 small butternut squash,
peeled, seeded, and cut
into wedges
1 tsp fresh thyme leaves
salt and black pepper

METHOD

Melt the butter in a medium-sized saucepan, add in the diced onion and cook over a very low heat for 5-6 minutes until completely softened. Mix in the lemon zest, the freshly chopped herbs and the soft white breadcrumbs. Season this mixture lightly. Allow to cool.

Preheat the oven to 200°C/400°F/Gas Mark 6.

Stuff the cavity of the chicken with the cold stuffing, then add half a lemon, both to keep the stuffing in place and for additional flavour. Place the chicken onto a roasting tray. Loosen the skin of the chicken and taking a little additional butter gently massage the butter into the breasts under the skin of the chicken. Sprinkle a little bit of salt and cracked black pepper over the skin.

Transfer the chicken to the oven and roast for 15-20 minutes. At this stage, reduce the temperature of the oven to 160°C/325°F/Gas Mark 3 and cook for a further hour or until the juices run clear out of the chicken. The flesh, particularly on the legs and thighs, should feel tender indicating that the bird is cooked.

For the roasted root vegetables: Parboil all of the vegetables, separately, and then place on a roasting tray with some fresh thyme and roast for 20-30 minutes until the vegetables are completely tender and caramelized. I normally use a little butter or duck fat to roast them off as this gives them a nice shine and extra flavour. Season with salt and pepper.

SERVES 4

Thai Coconut Chicken Curry with Pilau Rice

To make sure you get lovely fluffy rice, wash it several times in cold water, then leave to soak for about 30 minutes in fresh cold water. If you don't have time for this, place in a sieve and wash under the cold tap for a minute.

INGREDIENTS

4 chicken breasts, shredded very thinly
½ green pepper
½ red pepper
1 red onion
2 tbsp coconut oil or sunflower oil
2 tsp red curry paste
400ml/14fl oz/1¾ cups coconut milk
100ml/3½fl oz/scant ½ cup chicken stock, warmed
2 kaffir lime leaves
1 tbsp mango chutney, optional

Pilau rice
450g/1lb basmati rice
1 medium onion, finely chopped
large knob butter, plus extra to serve, optional
1 bay leaf
600ml/1 pint/2⅔ cups hot chicken stock, vegetable stock or water
salt

METHOD

Slice the peppers and red onion thinly. Heat the oil in a deep wide-based pan. Add in the finely sliced chicken and cook very quickly for approximately 2 minutes.

Next add the sliced and prepared vegetables and cook quickly for another moment or two on a very high heat.

Add the red curry paste to the pan and fry this for 1-2 minutes until the chicken and vegetables are all fully coated with the paste. Pour the coconut milk into the pan, add the chicken stock, kaffir lime leaves and the mango chutney at this stage. Cover the pan and allow this to simmer for 10-15 minutes over a medium heat.

When the curry is cooked, serve it in a large bowl with some pilau rice.

Pilau rice
In a frying pan, cook the onion in the butter over a medium heat for around 5 minutes until softened. Add the bay leaves and cook for a couple more minutes. Add the rice and stir until the grains are coated in the butter before stirring in the stock or water and salt.

Bring to the boil and then cover with a tight-fitting lid. If the lid isn't tight enough, cover the pan with aluminium foil before putting the lid on. Turn the heat down low and leave to cook for 10 minutes before turning off the heat. Don't remove the lid, just leave the rice to continue cooking in the pan for about 5 minutes until you're ready to serve.

The rice should have absorbed all the water and will just need fluffing up with a fork. Add a knob of butter – optional but delicious – before serving.

SERVES 4-6

Creamy Forest Mushroom & Free Range Chicken Pie

Simply delicious and deliciously simple to make. You can follow my recipe to make one large pie or several little individual pies.

INGREDIENTS

4 large chicken breasts, diced
25g/1oz/2 tbsp butter
1 leek, thinly sliced or
1 large onion
3 garlic cloves, crushed
200g/7oz forest mushrooms
25g/1oz/¼ cup, firmly
packed plain flour
75ml/2½fl oz/5 tbsp
white wine
55g/2oz/½ cup cheddar cheese,
grated
400ml/14fl oz/1¾ cups milk

Topping
1 sheet of puff pastry,
ready rolled
1 egg yolk beaten with
2 tsp water, for egg wash

METHOD

Heat the butter in a large shallow saucepan and add a little bit of oil to stop the butter from burning. Add in the chicken and cook for 4-5 minutes. Add in the leeks, garlic and mushrooms at this stage together with a little seasoning.

After cooking for a further 5 minutes, sprinkle in the flour and use this to dry up any liquids in the pot and thicken the sauce. Pour in the white wine, cheese and the milk and allow the mixture to come to a gentle boil whilst stirring all the time. You could add a little cream as well if you're feeling naughty.

Simmer for 5-6 minutes and then transfer to a large casserole dish.

Neatly arrange the pastry on top. Brush the pastry lightly with a little egg wash glaze and bake in a preheated oven (190°C/375°F/ Gas Mark 5) for approximately 30 minutes. Serve with some dressed salad greens.

SERVES 4

Creamy Chicken & Black Pudding Pie

Use good-quality black pudding to enrich the flavour of this delicious pie, which is good enough to enjoy on its own, accompanied by a seasonal salad or some steamed vegetables.

INGREDIENTS

25g/1oz/2 tbsp butter
1 tbsp olive oil
4 large chicken breasts, diced
1 leek, thinly sliced
3 garlic cloves, crushed
200g/7oz forest mushrooms
200g/7oz black pudding
(blood sausage)
90ml/3fl oz/6 tbsp white wine
400ml/14fl oz/1¾ cups cream

Topping

2 sheets of puff pastry,
ready rolled
oil and flour, for dusting
1 egg yolk beaten with
2 tsp water, for egg wash

METHOD

Heat the butter in a large shallow saucepan with a drizzle of oil to prevent the butter from burning. Add in the chicken and cook for 4-5 minutes then add the leeks, garlic, mushrooms and black pudding. Add a little seasoning.

Pour in the white wine and cream, allowing the mixture to come to a gentle boil whilst stirring all the time. Simmer for 5-6 minutes until the liquid has reduced and thickened, then set aside for 30 minutes.

Preheat the oven to 180°C/350°F/Gas Mark 4. Meanwhile, prepare the pie dish by rubbing the edges with a little oil or butter and a dusting of flour. Roll out 1 sheet of pastry on a lightly floured surface, then using the dish base as a template cut around the base and place the cut disc of pastry inside the dish.

Use the remaining pastry to line the edges of the dish then pour in the cooled mixture. Place the top sheet of puff pastry over the dish, and brush with egg wash, trim as necessary.

Place in the preheated oven and bake for approximately 30-40 minutes. Serve immediately.

THE PUB THAT SAILED TO AMERICA

Ballyknockan, County Wicklow, Ireland.
Paul Nolan: Smoke and Mirrors

The school bus wound its way along the narrow country roads every morning through rain, snow or sunshine (though mostly rain). It took an hour or so to get all the way from Ballyknockan village in County Wicklow, around the Poulaphouca reservoir and into Dublin. There was just one bus there and back, each day. If the young Paul Nolan missed it after school, or if it was simply full up, he would have to wait to get a lift from his father, Frank Nolan. And that could be any time between 6 p.m. and 2 a.m. the following morning. Frank was often working late for the marketing department at Guinness in Dublin and, given the unreliability of the bus, Paul ended up spending hours after school on the sets of advertising shoots. It was on one such shoot that his career in marketing began with an appearance in an ad that featured a St. Patrick's Day parade. Paul was there, in the thick of it, but due to the restrictions of using children in ads for alcohol, his face could not be shown. He appeared carrying a currach – a type of Irish row boat—over his head.

"Guinness back then," says Paul, "was famous for looking after people really well. If you got into Guinness, you were pretty much set up for life."

Guinness was a major employer in Dublin, and the company provided pension plans, health services and housing for its people early in its history. At one point, the company estimated that one in 30 people in Dublin were dependent on Guinness for their livelihood. "They had a big swimming pool at the brewery at St. James's Gate, as well as sports grounds so, as a child, Guinness played a big part in our lives," Paul remembers.

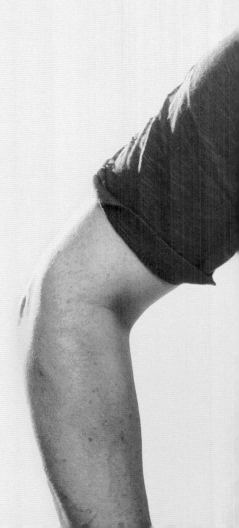

The presence of Guinness back in the family home in Ballyknockan was felt most strongly when his father began working at the laboratory dedicated to maintaining the quality of the beer that was sent all over the world. Inevitably a lot of beer found its way home. Paul grew up with Guinness literally running through his veins.

"We would have it like you would have a glass of cola at the table with meals. From when we were about 12 or 13 years old we were allowed to drink it." This relaxed approach to alcohol led to Paul's puzzlement over fellow teens' lack of access to beer. "I didn't get it. When other fellas were trying to get beer, I was walking around saying 'what's the big deal?'"

In the 1970s and early '80s, Guinness was known worldwide for its epic advertising campaigns. It was one of the few Irish companies that had made it to the world stage as a truly global brand, and Irish people were naturally very proud of it. This was at a time when the Irish economy was in dire straits and there were few notable examples of Irish success. So when his father began working for Guinness's marketing department, his part in that success made a huge impression on Paul.

After college, Paul went to work in the advertising industry in Dublin and, while he was building his career, he was aware that his father was looking into replicating the Irish pub experience abroad with Guinness.

"One of the things that really intrigued Guinness was the phenomenon of the Americans who came to Ireland, drank copious amounts of Guinness, then went home and drank it at local bars. Guinness realized that they were buying much more than just beer and were using the drink as a way of identifying with their Irishness."

Paul was also quick to see the impact that the success of the Irish soccer team had on raising the profile of Ireland and of Guinness. "Europeans suddenly saw what Irishness was all about. When the Ireland team played a match in Stuttgart or Rome, you had maybe 30,000 Irish soccer fans arriving in a city. The city would brace itself for trouble but, within a few days, the policemen were sitting down drinking with the fans."

It is not surprising then that Paul seized the opportunity to work with the brand development firm that was dedicated to establishing Irish pubs abroad—the Irish Pub Company – and spent seven years there. It was there that he met his business partner, John Cooke, working closely with McNally Design, the consultancy arm of the IPC. Wherever Paul went, his eye was always drawn to the best Irish pub in town.

"On a main street in Germany you could have a good German pub and a good Irish pub, and the Irish pub would be doing triple the volume of the German one," he explains.

The American market was probably the last market in the developed world to embrace the authentic Irish pub concept because in America, unlike elsewhere in the world, there were already established Irish bars. But these drinking establishments had very little in common with pubs back home in Ireland. In Paul's words, "They involved someone throwing a shamrock on the wall and calling it 'Murphy's' but, for all intents and purposes, it remained an American bar."

To get across the difference between an authentic Irish pub and an Irish bar in America, the Irish Pub Company opened a concept called Fado in Atlanta, Georgia. Fado became a phenomenal success with its true Irish pub atmosphere.

With the success of Fado, Paul and John began considering the idea of creating an Irish pub the size of a Planet Hollywood. Irish pubs back home tended to cover about 10,000 square feet because of the scale of existing historic buildings in Ireland. What if an Irish pub were built to cover 20,000-30,000 square feet?

 "When you get to those sizes, you can spend money on fantastic interiors, great staff and do stuff with food that had never been done before," Paul says.

At that time, in the 1990s, Ireland was shaking off its economic troubles and a new Irish cuisine was emerging from Irish chefs who created dishes with fresh flair using local, natural ingredients. Until then, the typical Irish pub did not have a reputation for good food, to put it mildly. The time was right to find a chef who would embrace the challenge of revolutionizing pub food. It was at this point that John Cooke called Kevin Dundon, and the three eventual owners of Raglan Road began their collaboration.

Before Orlando entered the picture, they decided there was no better place than Las Vegas to create a bigger and bolder Irish pub experience. When Paul and John approached New York-New York for the Irish Pub Company, casinos were beginning to make good money from food and beverage offerings and were open to new restaurant concepts. Tom McCartney, the casino manager for New York-New York, was familiar with the legend of the "Nine Fine Irishmen"—the eventual name of the pub—and wanted their story to be the inspiration for the design.

"We started off with what was going to be a small Irish pub in Vegas," Paul explains. "We expressed our thoughts about making it bigger and better and eventually created this big business concept." Nine Fine Irishmen opened in 2003 and is a great success. John Redmond, president of MGM at the time, said, "It's the only place in all our venues where you can have a grandfather talking at the bar with his grandson, and both are happy to be there."

When Disney officials visited Nine Fine Irishmen, they liked the way the pub was run as a community centre.

"Going to the pub is a family thing in Ireland," explains Paul. "They are not exclusively hard drinking places, and that made Disney more amenable to it."

With a promising plan in place, John and Paul decided to pursue the opportunity to open their own Irish pub at a Disney site in Orlando, Florida or in California and left the Irish Pub Company to do so. They signed the deal with Disney on Christmas Eve 2004. The new pub, Raglan Road, would open nine months later at Downtown Disney Pleasure Island on the site of a former jazz club.

Paul, John and Kevin now had the opportunity to design an Irish pub from scratch.

"We wanted to recreate a classic Dublin pub, which meant a pub from the Victorian era with ornate design, lots of detailing and stained glass," Paul says. "An interior where the dark woodwork is handcrafted, there are tiled floors, and it's all very comfortable." For inspiration, the Irishmen chose their favourite Dublin pubs— places like the Palace Bar, The Long Hall and The Stag's Head. Then they sourced all the distinctively Irish interior fixtures and fittings directly from Ireland.

Raglan Road was the first pub in America to be owned, designed, built and managed by Irish people, and that's what differentiates its look and feel.

"We had been brought up in the Irish pub business, so we did not feel the need to hammer home the fact that Raglan Road was an Irish pub," Paul says, noting that the pub speaks for itself with décor that includes a number of genuine antique pieces from Ireland that were worked into the design. "Both bars are a couple of hundred years old. One is made from an old apothecary's shop salvaged in Dublin. You can open the drawers and still smell the essences of the old drugs."

Wooden paneling on the Raglan Road walls comes from old Victorian houses in Dublin that were being replaced or demolished. Everything in the pub is real, salvaged or made by traditional Irish craftsmen.

This attention to detail extends to the management of the pub.

"We recreate what really happens in a well-run Dublin pub," Paul says. More often than not, a pub in Ireland is a family business. When an Irish family opened a pub and it went well, they extended it into the back room, then upstairs, and frequently they bought the place next door. It's a process that gives Dublin pubs that distinctive warren of rooms and convivial atmosphere. "The owner knows everybody who walks into the bar and what they want to drink. He has to know whose drink is nearly empty, who is coming through the door, who is in a good mood and who is in a bad one and how to cheer them up. His livelihood depends on it." It was that deep, instinctive awareness of customer needs that the three Irishmen brought to the new pub.

"We deprogram our staff when they come to us," Paul says. "We try to get people to be themselves as they would if they were serving in a pub in Ireland."

That means no scripted welcome messages or "have a nice day" farewells for Raglan Road guests. Instead, staff members bring their personality to the show while always bearing in mind that they are not the stars—the customers are.

"Disney has done a great job entertaining guests before they even get to our door," Paul says, "so, at the very least, we have to maintain that high level of enjoyment or even take it a little bit higher."

We have now reached America on the road to Raglan Road. The pub is open to guests daily and continues to draw new fans from around the world. So how did Paul, John and Kevin decide to name their pub? To be sure, the "Raglan Road" moniker is invested with a backstory equal to its namesake.

Fish

Some people think of a fish as a tricky beast. Maybe it's the bones or the fact that it can be overcooked so easily but, whatever the reason, they're not willing to take the plunge and get their teeth into a fish dish. That's a real shame. Not only is fresh fish quick and easy to cook properly, it has one of the most beautiful and delicate of tastes. In Ireland, where the sea surrounds us, perhaps we're more used to handling fish and shellfish. For a gentle introduction to all things fishy, try my recipe for Chilli & Garlic Prawns, which really couldn't be simpler, or my Smoked Haddock Smokey, one of the most popular dishes ever on the Raglan Road menu (I took it off the menu at one point and diners forced me to put it back on!) Then try your hand at my Lemon Zest Crusted Cod, Cherry Vine Tomatoes & Broad Beans or my Pan Seared Fillet of Salmon with Citrus Salad & Herb Vinaigrette. Fish can be fancy or unfussy, but it doesn't have to be fiddly.

SERVES 4-6

Not Bleedin' Chowder

This recipe makes a really great soup, but you could also consider using this same mixture as the base for a seafood pasta or vol-au-vent or even for a fisherman's pie with savoury crumble topping, pastry or mashed potato. But however you use it, and whatever you do, remember: don't call it 'chowder'! I recommend using cod, haddock, salmon and smoked salmon, mussels and langoustines.

INGREDIENTS

2 celery stalks
1 leek, thinly sliced
1 carrot, diced finely
25g/1oz/2 tbsp butter
2 garlic cloves, crushed
2 sprigs thyme
25g/1oz/¼ cup, firmly
packed plain flour
75ml/2½fl oz/5 tbsp
white wine
400ml/14fl oz/1¾ cups
fish stock
200ml/7fl oz/generous
¾ cup cream
600g/1lb 8oz selection
of fish and shellfish
1 tsp tarragon, chopped
20ml/¾fl oz/4 tsp Pernod
salt and pepper

METHOD

Slice and dice up the vegetables into bite-size pieces and sauté off in the butter with garlic and thyme until they are glazed but without colour.

Next, mix the flour into the vegetable base and use it to coat the vegetables, lightly, and to dry up any juices in the pan.

Add in the white wine, fish stock and cream and allow the vegetables to cook out slightly. Cook this mixture out. At this stage you can leave things to cool down and reheat it later before adding the fish.

When the vegetables have softened, add in the fish and shellfish. At this stage try not to stir the soup too much, as this will cause the fish to break up. Cook, very gently, for 5-6 minutes just until the fish is cooked.

When the fish is lightly poached, add in some freshly chopped tarragon and that shot of Pernod which gives the soup its aniseed flavour. Serve immediately.

SERVES 4

Lemon Zest Crusted Cod, Cherry Vine Tomatoes & Broad Beans

You can substitute salmon, hake or haddock for the cod if you prefer them to cod.

INGREDIENTS

4 portions of cod fillet,
175g/6oz each
3 lemons, 2 cut into wedges
100g/3½oz/scant ½ cup butter
200g/7oz/4 cups fresh
breadcrumbs
20g/¾oz/scant ¼ cup
Parmesan, grated
2 tbsp chopped fresh herbs,
such as parsley and oregano
2 sprigs of thyme
12 cherry tomatoes
on the vine
450g/1lb potatoes, washed,
scrubbed and peeled
60ml/2fl oz/generous
⅜ cup cream
350g/12oz/1½ cups butter
400g/14oz fresh broad
beans, unskinned
salt and pepper

METHOD

Preheat the oven to 180°C/350°F/ Gas Mark 4.

Grate and then juice one of the lemons. Melt 100g/3½oz/scant ½ cup butter in a saucepan and stir in the lemon zest, breadcrumbs, Parmesan cheese, chopped herbs and seasoning. Then remove and allow to cool for a few of minutes.

Place fish on a roasting tray and season. Divide the breadcrumb topping between the portions of fish and press onto the top of each. Add lemon wedges and cherry tomatoes around the fish. Bake for 20 minutes until topping is crunchy. Boil potatoes for 15-20 minutes. Place through a potato ricer to remove any lumps then add the cream, 100g/3½oz/scant ½ cup butter, and season. Keep warm until required.

Place a pan of water over a high heat and have a bowl of iced water ready on the side. Once the pan of water has reached boiling point, add the broad beans and blanch for 1–2 minutes. Remove from the heat and strain. Transfer the broad beans into the iced water. This will stop the cooking process. Remove the skins from the broad beans.

Pour the lemon juice into a small pan and heat gently. Remove from the heat, then add 150g/5½oz/ scant ¾ cup butter in small cubes a little at a time, stirring continuously with a small whisk. Melt 20g/¾oz/scant 2 tablespoons butter in a small pan and add the broad beans, saute gently for 2–3 minutes.

DUBLIN'S NOTORIOUS PRAWN STARS

What could be better than buying a catch of Dublin Bay prawns fresh off the boat that morning, tearing off the shells, adding a squirt of lemon, some garlic butter and frying them gently for a few minutes. Eat them with your fingers so you don't miss out on the mouth-watering juices.

But while you're thinking about enjoying Dublin's coolest crustacean, our very own homegrown prawn star, we've got a confession to make. They're not prawns, but rather, slim pinkish lobsters.

The truth is this: what we call Dublin Bay prawns have quite a few aliases including the Norway lobster, the langoustine and scampi as well as the more technical Nephrops norvegicus. So many names, indeed, that you might start to wonder if there's something fishy going on.

And you would be right because, not only are Dublin Bay "prawns" known by a wide variety of other names, they aren't actually from Dublin Bay. The prawn can be found in the Atlantic from as far north as freezing Iceland down to sunny Morocco and all over the Mediterranean.

Claws for Thought

In fact, the only place the little lobster doesn't hang out is Dublin Bay. It's never set a claw, leg or tail in it. How exactly it got the name is not known. It may be that the name stuck after it was being brought ashore by fishermen here and bought on the shores of Dublin Bay.

So, back to the Dublin Bay prawn. Not a prawn. Not from Dublin Bay. But who cares what it's called or where it's from as long as it's fresh and tasty? Pass the salt, please...

"It was a bold
man who ate the
first oyster."

Jonathan Swift (Irish satirist)

Traditional Battered Fish with Chunky Chips

Nothing beats the crispy crunch and the delicate flavour of batter-fried fish. This is my recipe for a really crunchy batter.

INGREDIENTS

4 portions fresh cod –
be sure the fillets are
boneless and skinless
200g/7oz/1¾ cups, firmly
packed plain flour, plus
extra for dusting
75g/2½oz/generous
½ cup cornflour
1 tsp salt and pepper mix
250ml/9fl oz/scant 1¼ cups
lager, Harp or Budweiser
100ml/3½fl oz/scant
½ cup soda water
4 wedges of lemon

chips
4 large potatoes

Tartar sauce
250g/9oz mayonnaise
2 tbsp gherkins, chopped
1 tsp capers
2 shallots, finely diced
1 tbsp parsley,
freshly chopped
juice of 1 lemon
½ tsp Dijon mustard

METHOD

Sift the flour and cornflour into a bowl with the salt and pepper to make the beer batter. Make a well in the centre and pour the lager and soda water into it. Whisk the liquid ingredients together and then gradually whisk in the flour mixture until you have achieved a smooth batter. Store in the fridge.

Cut the fish into smaller pieces, if you prefer, or leave it large pieces. Dust the strips of fish in a light coating of flour and then dredge in the batter, shaking off any excess. Deep-fry for about 5 minutes or until cooked through. Do this in batches depending on the size of your fryer. If you're cooking larger pieces of fish, start cooking it in the fryer and then transfer to the oven to finish cooking.

Wash and peel the potatoes. Cut them into thick cut chips and store in water until required.

Deep fry in hot oil at 180°C/350°F/Gas Mark 4 until fully cooked.

Serve the fish and chips in little cones made from rolled newspaper, and a wedge of lemon and enjoy.

Tartar sauce
Put the mayonnaise into a large mixing bowl. Add the chopped gherkins, capers, shallots and parsley and lemon juice. Next mix in the Dijon mustard and mix it in really well. Store until needed. Serve as an accompaniment to the fish.

SERVES 4

Pan Seared Fillet of Salmon with Citrus Salad & Herb Vinaigrette

Salmon is often referred as the 'steak of the sea'. It's high in Omega-3 fatty acids which have proven health benefits.

INGREDIENTS

4 salmon fillets, approx.
150-175g/5½–6oz each
75ml/2½fl oz/5 tbsp
white wine
2-3 sprigs fresh dill or
flat-leaf parsley
3 lemons, grated zest
and juice
5 tbsp olive oil
1 lime, grated zest and juice
1 tsp honey
1 tbsp mint, freshly chopped
500g/1lb 2oz baby
garden leaves
1 orange segmented,
peeled and pith removed
salt and pepper
50g/1¾oz/½ cup flaked
almonds, toasted

METHOD

Preheat the oven to 180˚C/350˚F/ Gas Mark 4.

To prepare a marinade for the salmon, first pour the wine into a bowl and add the herbs, the zest and juice of one lemon, 1 tablespoon of olive oil and some seasoning. Place the salmon fillets in the bowl and leave to marinade for 20-30 minutes.

Preheat a large non-stick pan. When the pan is hot, place the salmon, skin side down, in the pan. Cook for 2-5 minutes on a medium heat on each side until golden brown, then either place the pan in the oven for an extra 15 minutes or continue on the stovetop on a medium to low heat for 20 minutes.

In the meantime, make the vinaigrette by combining the zest and juice of 1 lemon and 1 lime in a small bowl. Add the honey, seasoning, herbs and olive oil, whisk until well combined.

Dress the baby garden leaves with the vinaigrette, then add the segmented orange and the toasted almond. Divide the salad between 4 plates and place a slice of salmon on each. Enjoy the fish hot or cold.

THE CHIPPER

Pearse Street, Dublin, Ireland.
Giuseppe Cervi: Chipper Maestro.

When the Irish owners of Raglan Road shipped the pub from Ireland where it was built, they remembered to include a "chipper"—Cookes of Dublin. What's a "chipper," you may wonder? A chipper is an establishment serving freshly cooked food, especially fried fish in batter and chips prepared for takeout or "to go." Cookes has been serving food this way to Dubliners for three generations. All over Ireland, it's traditional to pop into a chipper to pick up fish and chips or a battered burger and chips to take home for dinner or to eat on the street out of a newspaper wrapping. Irish chips, we should explain, are similar to American "fries" except that they're wider and thicker. What many don't know is that there's an intriguing Italian involvement in the growth of chippers in Ireland. Enter a young Italian named Giuseppe Cervi.

Legend has it that Giuseppe was on a boat for America that stopped in Cobh in County Cork in the 1880s. Giuseppe decided to leave ship at Cobh and ended up in Dublin where he worked as a labourer until he had enough money to buy a handcart and a coal-fired cooker. He started selling chips outside pubs. Business boomed. Soon, he could afford to open a shop believed to be the first chipper in Dublin close to Trinity College Dublin. Giuseppe's wife struggled with her English, so she would point to customer orders before they paid. "Uno di questo, uno do quello?" she would say. "One of this, one of that?" Today, you can still hear Dubliners use a popular mistranslation of this phrase – "one and one"—to order cod and chips. Or so the story goes.

By 1909, Giuseppe's success had inspired the opening of 19 more chippers in Dublin. What is extraordinary about this expansion is that almost all of the Italian families who opened the chippers came from the same small rural villages in the south of Italy. This migration to Ireland is reflected in the names of the chippers. Names like Macaris, Borzas and Caffellos, Italian families who are still serving Irish families their favourite take-away food today.

Chilli & Garlic Prawns

Panfried, grilled, or barbecued… Prawns always taste absolutely fab.
And never so much as when they're dressed up with garlic and chilli.
The perfect starter, finger food or tapas dish. Indulge and enjoy!

INGREDIENTS

500g/1lb 2oz king prawn tails, peeled and uncooked
1 red chilli
zest and juice of 1 lemon
2 garlic cloves, chopped
50g/1¾oz/scant 2 tbsp butter
100g/3½oz fresh coriander
1 tbsp olive oil
arugula leaves, washed
crostini bread, to serve

METHOD

To prepare the chilli, cut it in half lengthways, then scrape out and discard the seeds. Cut each half into fine strips, lengthways, and then cut again, across the strips, to get very fine dice.

Put the chilli, lemon zest, garlic, butter, and half the coriander together in a bowl. Combine until smooth to form a garlic and chilli butter.

When ready, heat the pan with oil over high heat and add the prawn tails. Pan fry for 1-2 minutes until they are pink and cooked, add the garlic and chilli butter. Let melt the butter on to the prawns, then toss to cover them completely in butter. Add the juice of the lemon and the rest of the fresh coriander.

Serve the prawns on a bed of arugula with crostini bread.

SERVES 4-6

Salmon Coulibiac

Coulibiac is a French adaptation of a savoury Russian recipe often made in loaf form. You can use smoked cod or haddock as an alternative to salmon.

INGREDIENTS

600g/1lb 5oz side of
salmon, skin removed
225g/8oz mushrooms,
thinly sliced
25g/1oz/2 tbsp butter
2 sheets puff pastry
1 egg yolk beaten with
2 tsp water, for egg wash
400g/14oz spinach,
sautéed and drained
2 eggs, hardboiled and peeled
2 shallots, thinly sliced
1 tbsp fresh dill
1 tsp lemon thyme
salt and freshly ground
black pepper

Hollandaise sauce
225g/8oz/1 cup butter,
melted completely
1 tsp white wine vinegar
or lemon juice
4 tsp boiling water, if required
3 large egg yolks
ground white pepper

METHOD

Preheat the oven to 180°C/350°F/ Gas Mark 4. Sauté the mushrooms in some butter, then remove and pat dry with kitchen paper. Roll out the two sheets of pastry on a lightly floured surface and brush the pastry with egg wash. Place the spinach on to the pastry, leaving approximately 2.5cm/1 inch around the edge before placing the sautéed mushrooms on top. Lay the salmon over the mushrooms and season with salt and pepper.

In a separate bowl mix the eggs and shallots, then place this mixture on top of the salmon. Sprinkle with the herbs, then brush the edges of the pastry with the egg wash. Place the top sheet of pastry on top of the salmon, then seal tightly to the bottom sheet. Transfer to a baking sheet and place in the preheated oven for 30–35 minutes before removing. Allow to stand for 15 minutes.

In the meantime to make your hollandaise sauce, firstly melt the butter in a saucepan over a gentle heat. Remove the saucepan from the heat. In a separate saucepan, heat some water and place a glass or stainless steel bowl on the surface so that it floats. Pour the white wine vinegar and lemon juice into the bowl, then add the egg yolks and beat continuously until you get a light and creamy consistency.

You need to be very careful at this stage because the line between creamy and scrambled is a very fine one. Remove the bowl from the water, then pour in the melted butter, but don't stop whisking!

If, after adding all the butter, the sauce is still a little bit too thick for your liking whisk in some boiling water and a squeeze of lemon. Season to taste. Place the coulibiac onto a serving platter, and serve with Hollandaise sauce.

MARRIED TO THE PUB

Port Douglas, Queensland, Australia.
Sean Griffin: Husband
Lorraine Gorham: Wife

James Mulligan, originally from County Down in Ireland, missed out on the gold rushes at Ballarat and Gympie in northeast Australia but the third time was the charm for the prospector. He finally discovered gold at Hodgkinson River in Far North Queensland and, in 1877, the town of Port Douglas was established to cater to the hundreds of hopefuls who began to flock to the site of this latest big find. More than 130 years later, in very different circumstances, this tiny town, thousands of miles from Ireland, was the meeting place for two young Irish people – Sean Griffin and Lorraine Gorham. The two were traveling in Australia after both studied hotel and catering management at the Galway-Mayo Institute of Technology in Ireland, but it was at Port Douglas in September 2000 that their friendship and soon-to-be romance began.

Sean, originally from Glenbeigh, a village in County Kerry, grew up on a farm. His father was a plasterer who also worked the farm while his mother had a home-baking business for about 10 years. He used to come home from school and, whenever his mother worked long hours in the bakery – often for 12 hours a day, he would start cooking the family dinner. Sean discovered that he loved cooking and food, so he considered a career as a chef before deciding, instead, to study hotel management.

Lorraine is from Belmullet, County Mayo in the west of Ireland and comes from a family of eight children. Her father, like Sean's, was a plasterer, and her family's wanderlust led to several siblings' moves to different parts of the world. Lorraine has a brother in Malaysia, another in Nigeria, and a sister in New Zealand.

Although she and Sean both come from the west of Ireland, have fathers who worked as plasterers and studied the same course at Galway, she describes herself as "his polar opposite – the chalk to his cheese."

One reason they both studied the course in hotel and catering management was so they could spend time abroad. Like generations of Irish people before them, they emigrated. First, Sean headed for Las Vegas to work at Nine Fine Irishmen, then both of them joined Raglan Road as joint managers when the pub opened in 2005. "In order to hire Sean, they had to hire me," says Lorraine. The two married in 2009.

At first, they were awed by Paul's and John's vast pub-and-restaurant-business knowledge.

"It can be quite intimidating when you're just starting your career and you're working for people who seem to know everything," Lorraine says.

"John would scare the living daylights out of you, initially," admits Sean. "He'd be talking about profit and loss accounts one minute, then switch effortlessly to how you make the perfect 'beurre blanc,' then shift to discussing the air conditioning units we would need in the pub. How the hell did he know all this stuff?" The two say that they have learned more from John and Paul than they would have learned if they had stayed in college for the next 20 years.

The couple knew from the very start that the training they gave their staff would be crucial. The most important element is a deep immersion in Irish culture.

"They love the history that we bring to Raglan Road as Irish people – it's different from everything else in the area," they say. When the staff greets them by asking, "What's the craic (news or gossip)?" or when they overhear them using phrases like "that's grand" to each other, they know the training is working.

Training staff members to use their instincts with guests is important, because there is no script.

"We don't want servers to go up to people and robotically say, 'Hello, my name is Geraldo, I'll be your server, today,'" Lorraine says. "We teach them to 'read' a table, to establish the mood of the people." The important thing, she says, is that servers "don't go in, all guns blazing, with a 'Top o' the morning' and acting like Mr. Irish, but take time to judge the feeling and respond appropriately."

Despite the size of Raglan Road, Sean and Lorraine try to run it like a cozy local pub. "To a publican back in Ireland," Sean says, "the pub is their home; it's their world; it's their life. It means something."

Sean and Lorraine have discovered that some people have strange ideas of what life is like in contemporary Ireland. One day, a group asked Lorraine if she had ever seen a leprechaun in real life. At one table, a child was chewing gum and his family offered Sean a stick and asked whether they had chewing gum back in Ireland. The strangest complaint they have heard was from a man who asked why there was no goat in his goat's cheese salad?

Raglan Road prides itself on providing Irish drinks and cuisine as they might actually be served in Ireland, but this can sometimes cause problems.

"We've had a few people storm out of here asking how we can call ourselves an Irish pub when we don't serve corned beef and cabbage," says Sean, although the dish actually is an American creation and is almost unheard of in Ireland. Patrons sometimes ask servers for green beer or for a shamrock on top of a pint of Guinness, even though these are American celebratory specialties not common in Ireland.

The fact that the pub represents the living, breathing, contemporary Ireland of the 21st century also can prompt disbelief.

Who could play that role? A musician? A storyteller? A priest?

"We have things like chicken curry and brown soda bread on the menu, and some people have said, 'that's not Irish,' as if they had found us out in some kind of deception," Lorraine says. Sometimes, actual second- or third-generation Irish people even question the pair about Raglan Road's contemporary Irish cuisine, "even though we were both born and raised in Ireland. I'm still not sure they believe us sometimes."

Sean and Lorraine miss their homeland, friends and families, and visit when they can. They say you have to leave Ireland in order to appreciate the country's treasures, which include the natural warmth of Irish people. "I remember going through a toll booth on my way to the airport one morning and, as the man at the booth handed me my change, he said, 'God bless,' and he meant it. You cannot beat that intimate feeling about Ireland," Lorraine says.

The next best thing, perhaps, is recreating it every day in a small corner of Florida. To do that, even with Irish owners and an Irish husband-and-wife team to run it, Raglan Road needs something extra – a host who ensures that every guest who comes through the doors has a really great time. Who could play that role? A musician? A storyteller? A priest? How about all three rolled into one? Next, we'll meet Jay Shanahan.

Desserts

You should always leave room for dessert! Fruit desserts, creamy desserts, indulgent desserts, healthy desserts... no meal would be complete without a happy ending.

When I was growing up, we always had a dessert on Sunday, like most families at the time. It was usually some type of baked or steamed pudding. By the end of the meal, the bowl would be licked clean.

This chapter gathers together my favored and preferred dessert recipes that I've encountered down the years. A lot of them are real classics that everyone should try.

Every September, the tiny town of Lisdoonvarna in County Clare—population 800 or so—holds a matchmaking festival that lasts a month. It attracts 40,000 visitors from around the world, making it Europe's largest singles event. On the face of it, it's rather astonishing that a small Irish town should have such a large role in bringing people together in holy matrimony.

But the town does have a history. It became an unlikely tourist attraction after 1751 when Limerick surgeon Sylvester O'Halloran—who later founded the Royal College of Surgeons—discovered and promoted the beneficial effects of its mineral waters for drinking and bathing. The iron, sulphur, iodine and magnesium in the waters were reputed to relieve the symptoms of rheumatism and glandular fever.

The popularity of the mineral springs drew large numbers of people to the spa in Lisdoonvarna. That, in turn, led to the matchmaking tradition. September was the most popular month because once crops were harvested, bachelor farmers in their 40s and 50s had time to leave the fields and rush to Lisdoonvarna to find a wife. Men living on isolated farms often delayed marriage while waiting to inherit land from their elderly parents and, by the time the land was theirs, they had few remaining contacts with suitable local women and needed the help of a matchmaker. The tradition continued well into the 1920s when the town was described as a place "where parish priests pretend to be sober and bank clerks pretend to be drunk."

The Last Matchmaker?

Willie Daly is one of the last remaining traditional matchmakers in Ireland. He has been weaving his matrimonial magic from The Matchmaker Bar in Lisdoonvarna for roughly 30 years, keeping his research on available singletons in a large, worn book scribbled with many insights. His father and grandfather also practiced the art, and now his daughter Claire has become the fourth Daly generation to play cupid.

Many people from around the world, and not just farmers, prefer to travel to the town rather than trust online dating sites. They queue patiently, waiting to describe their perfect match to Willie, hoping he can fix them up. If they don't find Mr. or Miss Right at the set dances or one of the tiny town's 13 pubs, they certainly have a lot of fun trying.

"It's the only thing sexier than a sexy woman. A sexy woman cooking sausages."

Roddy Doyle (Irish novelist in his novel "Paula Spencer")

Hot Desserts

These hot desserts bring back memories of my Irish childhood. There are the classic comfort food of old-fashioned favourites like my Traditional Bread & Butter Pudding and my Sticky Toffee Pudding with Butterscotch Sauce, which I ate on cold, rainy winter evenings as a kid. Hot and hearty, these puddings are not for the faint hearted. But I've included a splash of grown-up sophistication in recipes like my Roasted Peaches with mascarpone and my Indulgent Chocolate Fondants with Guinness Ice Cream, which are sure to be the stars of any dinner party.

SERVES 4

Roasted Peaches with Mascarpone

Peaches are not only great fresh, they're also fantastic in both sweet and savoury dishes too.

INGREDIENTS

4 ripe peaches
50g/1¾oz/¼ cup, firmly
packed muscovado sugar
20g/¾oz/scant 2 tbsp butter
50ml/1¾fl oz/scant
¼ cup orange juice
1 vanilla pod, optional

To serve
mascarpone

METHOD

Begin by placing the pan on the heated barbecue. Add the muscovado sugar, butter and orange juice and allow to caramelise. Halve the peaches, removing the stones. Split the vanilla pod lengthways. Add the peaches and vanilla pod to the caramelised juices. Don't be afraid to use the pan on the barbecue as if you were using a stove. Baste peaches well in the pan juices for 6-8 minutes until softened.

Remove carefully and serve immediately with a generous scoop of mascarpone on top.

SERVES 4-6

Traditional Bread & Butter Pudding

This is a pudding that can be made in so many different and delicious ways. I prefer this classic soft set with its wonderful buttery top. But it's also fabulous made with day-old brioche or croissants instead of the traditional white sliced bread.

INGREDIENTS

85g/3oz/generous ⅓ cup butter, at room temperature
12 slices medium white bread
55g/2oz/generous ⅓ cup raisins
300ml/10fl oz/ 1⅓ cups cream
300ml/10fl oz/1⅓ cups milk
4 eggs
85g/3oz/scant ½ cup, firmly packed superfine sugar
½ tsp ground cinnamon

METHOD

Generously butter an ovenproof dish. Remove the crusts from the bread and using the remaining butter coat both sides, and then cut each slice into quarters to form triangles.

Arrange a single layer of the bread triangles, overlapping slightly in the bottom of the buttered dish. Scatter over some of the raisins, then place a second layer of the bread triangles on top and scatter over the remaining raisins. Press down gently with a fish slice or spatula.

To make the custard, heat the cream and milk in a pan until it almost comes to the boil. Remove from the heat. Meanwhile, whisk together the eggs, sugar and ground cinnamon in a large heatproof bowl set over a pan of simmering water until thickened and the whisk leaves a trail in the mixture. Remove from the heat and beat in the cream and milk mixture until well combined. Pour two-thirds of the custard over the layered bread triangles and leave to stand for about 30 minutes or until the bread has soaked up all of the custard.

Preheat the oven to 180°C/150°F/ Gas Mark 4. Pour the remaining custard over the soaked bread and butter triangles and arrange the remaining bread triangles on top. Press down firmly with a fish slice so that the custard comes halfway up the bread triangles. Bake for 30-35 minutes until the custard is just set and the top is golden brown.

To serve, bring the bread and butter pudding straight to the table and have a jug of custard ready to hand around so that everyone can help themselves to a good slosh of it.

Indulgent Chocolate Fondants with Guinness Ice-Cream

A good chocolate fondant is hot and intense with a meltingly soft centre.

INGREDIENTS

115g/4oz/½ cup butter
200g/7oz/7 squares dark
chocolate, broken into pieces
3 eggs, separated
115g/4oz/½ cup, firmly
packed superfine sugar
25g/1oz/¼ cup, firmly
packed plain flour
cream, to serve

Ice cream
600ml/1 pint/
2⅔ cups Guinness
600ml/1 pint/
2⅔ cups cream
1 vanilla pod,
split lengthways
6 egg yolks
175g/6oz/⅞ cup
superfine sugar

METHOD

Preheat the oven to 180°C/150°F/ Gas Mark 4. Generously butter 4 pudding basins using 25g/1oz of butter.

Melt the chocolate in a heatproof bowl set over a pan of simmering water. Remove from the heat and whisk in the remaining 85g/3oz/3/8 cup butter until melted. Set aside.

Whisk egg whites in a bowl until stiff peaks have formed. Whisk in half of the sugar, a third at a time, whisking well after each addition until stiff and very shiny.

In a separate bowl, beat the remaining sugar and egg yolks until pale and fluffy, then beat this mixture into the cooled chocolate and butter. Fold in the sifted flour. Fold in the meringue and fill basins two-thirds full. Bake on a tray for 12 minutes until well risen but still with a slight wobble in the middle. Leave to settle

Ice cream
Put Guinness into a large saucepan and bring to the boil. Reduce it to approximately 150ml/5fl oz/2/3 cup liquid. Put the cream and the vanilla pod onto a medium heat and bring to the boil. Remove from the heat and infuse with the vanilla.

Beat the egg yolks and sugar until thick and then add to the vanilla-infused cream (first remove the vanilla pod). Return the entire mixture to a saucepan over a gentle heat, stirring until the egg custard has thickened. If it coats the back of a spoon, then you're done. Pass through a sieve and whisk in the reserved Guinness. Churn in an ice cream machine or freezer. Serve.

Sticky Toffee Pudding

This rich date-filled sponge, drenched in butterscotch sauce, is not for the fainthearted. Cosy and comforting, it's hot dessert indulgence at its best.

INGREDIENTS

Toffee pudding
300g/10½oz/1¾ cups
pitted dates
300ml/10fl oz/1¼ cups water
10g/⅓ oz/2½ tsp bread soda
200g/7oz/⅞ cup butter
400g/14oz/1¾ cups,
firmly packed sugar
4 eggs
350g/12oz/3 cups,
firmly packed plain flour
scant 25g/1oz baking powder
2 tbsp milk
1 tsp vanilla essence

Butterscotch sauce
115g/4oz/½ cup butter
115g/4oz/½ cup brown sugar
150ml/5fl oz/⅔ cup cream

METHOD

Preheat the oven to 160°C/325°F/ Gas Mark 3.

Place the dates and water into a large saucepan and bring to the boil. Add the bread soda and allow to simmer for 10 minutes, then remove from the heat and allow to cool. Using a hand blender, blitz until you get a coarse consistency.

In the meantime, in a bowl cream together the butter and sugar using a dough mixer until light and fluffy. Add the eggs and sift in the flour and baking powder. Continue to mix until smooth. Pour in the milk and add the vanilla essence. Add in the cooled date mixture and combine well.

Pour into a greased and pre-lined baking tray or individual cake moulds. Place in the preheated oven for 40 minutes for a large one or 20 minutes for the smaller individual moulds.

Butterscotch sauce
Melt the butter in a large saucepan, then add in the brown sugar. Allow this mixture to come to the boil. Be very careful at this stage, as the butter and sugar mixture is very hot and could burn if you get it on your skin. Add the cream and whisk continuously. Allow the mixture to come to a boil and then reduce to a gentle simmer. Cook for 8-10 minutes and then serve with the sticky toffee pudding and enjoy.

SERVES 4

Cherry Jubilée

This is a very simple dessert to make. You can use canned cherries if fresh cherries are not available for an even quicker dessert.

INGREDIENTS

450g/1 lb. whole bing cherries, pitted
100g/3½oz/scant ½ cup, firmly packed superfine sugar
2 strips orange zest
juice of ½ lemon
100ml/3½fl oz/scant
½ cup kirsch warmed
4 scoops vanilla ice cream
whipped cream (optional)

METHOD

Toss the pitted cherries, sugar, the orange zest and the lemon juice in a bowl.

Preheat a dry pan over a moderate heat and when hot toss the cherry mixture into it, place a cover over the pan and cook for 4-5 minutes until the sugar has dissolved. Remove the cover and cook a further 2 minutes until the fruit is softened and juicy.

Tilt the pan to the side and carefully pour the kirsch over the cherries, let the kirsch ignite, taking care to turn off your extractor fan and move flammable objects out of harm's way. Once the flame has extinguished, remove the cherries from the heat.

Scoop vanilla ice cream into large cocktail glasses or onto dessert dishes, then spoon the cherries and juices over the ice cream. Serve with some freshly whipped cream for ultimate indulgence.

AN IRISH BLESSING

Immigration, Florida, USA.
Jay Shanahan: Raglan Road's 'Man Of The House'

Jay Shanahan had left the priesthood, and he stood waiting his turn in line at U.S. Immigration. After 15 years as a priest, it had been hard to find work except for an unusual job here and there, especially in Ireland. Then an invitation to work in America came along. When Jay eventually got to the head of the queue and spoke to the immigration officer, the man took a long, hard look at him and his visa application. The officer then said, "Mr. Shanahan, I see you're coming to America as an entertainer? Your last job was as a funeral director? That is something of a quantum leap. Can you explain it?" "Not really," said Jay, "except to say that I felt my talents were better used on the living than the dead." The "living" turned out to be the guests of Raglan Road where he had been invited to come and "entertain," even though he was not sure exactly what he would be doing.

"I've had an interesting life, to put it mildly," says Jay. He was born one of six children in Waterford, not far from the Waterford Crystal factory. His first paid job was as a ghost on a ghost train in Tramore, County Waterford, where he had to run around tickling and frightening passengers. He was called to serve God, entered the seminary at age 19 in 1970 and was a priest for 15 years until he met Gail, who is now his wife. When he left the priesthood, it was with the blessings of the community of which he was a part. "It was like leaving a home, a family and a job all on the same day. I left, and I did not know where I was going to turn," Jay says.

His next job was working as a Dublin funeral director for a company that was part of the Fanagans group, formed in 1819. At the same time, Jay also worked as a course director for the Glasnevin Musical Society and did a bit of market work on the side. "I taught singing on Saturdays and sold Jane Russell Gourmet Sausages on occasional weekends working at fairs in Marlay Park and Farmleigh."

When Jay arrived at Raglan Road, Paul Nolan took him aside to explain his new duties: "For the coming year, I want you to do one thing only – BE IRISH." Jay's job was to operate the front of house and insure that guests were having a good time. "I had absolutely no knowledge of restaurants at all," Jay cheerfully admits. "I would support the servers by going between the tables, having a chat and making connections with people." Ironically, he remembers, the big question that customers asked at the time was "How did Ireland get so wealthy, so fast?" This was in 2005, when Raglan Road had just opened and before Irish property values plummeted, the banks crashed spectacularly and the Celtic Tiger was still raging over the Atlantic.

Jay's advantage in speaking to Raglan Road guests was that, as a priest back in Ireland, he had traveled the length and breadth of Ireland doing parish retreats, visiting nearly all of the 32 counties. So he knew the entire country intimately and could talk to Americans about where they might have family roots.

Jay also put himself in charge of the rest rooms to ensure they were spotlessly clean, which was a particular pet peeve of his. As a result, Paul jokingly used to refer to him as the Director of Restroom Operations. Walking the floor as Raglan Road's Fear a'Tí (far uh tee) or "man of the house," Jay entertained guests and was entertained by them.

"I remember a guy from Brooklyn, New York," he says, "who, in the course of conversation, told me he had been widowed twice." The man sat on a barstool, enjoying the entertainment and having a bite to eat. His first wife had died, he told Jay, when they were in the Catskills camping and she became poisoned after eating wild mushrooms she had picked. He was on his own for three years and then remarried. He was only married for eight months when tragedy struck again. "Goodness, that was tough," Jay said to him. "Do you mind my asking what happened?" The man looked at him and replied without hesitation, "She wouldn't eat the mushrooms."

Another guest was celebrating his golden wedding anniversary so Jay, who had just become engaged to his fiancée Gail, asked him the secret of a happy and harmonious marriage.

"The guy thought for a moment and said that the secret was to always give the woman the last word." Jay came back to his table a little while later, and they began talking about flowers. "What's your favourite flower?" he asked the man's wife. "I just love camellias," she said. Jay then said to the husband, "What's your favourite flower?" Before he could reply his wife answered for him, "He loves the magnolia." Quick as a flash, the man said to Jay, "That's exactly what I was talking about before."

Jay's duties were not confined to the tables. During evenings, he would take the stage at 7:30 p.m. and play for about 30 minutes as a warm-up to the band. "I played guitar and keyboards for sing-a-long songs to get the crowd going," he says. "Songs like 'Danny Boy' and 'The Town I Loved So Well,' but the one that people loved the most was 'Those Were The Days.'" The other song they often requested was the 'Unicorn Song,' the one in which God instructs Noah to build an ark and fill it full of animals, especially the unicorn, 'the loveliest of all.'"

In conversations with guests, Jay learned that they liked the stories behind the fittings in the pub. Jay would sometimes hand guests a T-shaped ceramic object and invite them to guess what it was. It was a hot water bottle that pre-dated rubber hot water bottles. A lot of the bric-a-brac on display in Raglan Road was familiar to Jay from rural Ireland but was intriguing to guests – items such as scales with metal weights in ounces and pictures on the walls of the pub rooms. One day, Jay went through all the fittings and bric-a-brac supplied by Chas the bric-a-brac king and began to weave a story about Ireland through the objects. This informal explanation became known as the "Jay Walk" and has been printed as a pub-tour brochure for guests.

"I used to love asking what they thought the dance floor area was, originally," he says. "They couldn't believe it had once been a pulpit in a church back in Ireland. I used to tell them that, in many ways, it symbolized the journey that Ireland had been on." The previous occupant of the dance floor, Jay used to say, had not experienced the same joy using it as the dancers now enjoyed, every night. Presumably, the Raglan Road audience also is more entertained.

Jay has since returned to Dublin and works as a regional coordinator of employment schemes in South Kilkenny, where he supervises 25 people who keep the cemeteries, schools and communal services in order. Jay and Gail are now married with a child named Ella. "We will never be wealthy," Jay says, "but, by God, we're rich."

Let us leave Jay on that note and take his "Jay Walk" journey through Raglan Road.

JAY WALKING

'Raglan Road', Florida, USA.
Jay Shanahan: 'Fear a'Tí'

The first person to bring together all the stories from Raglan Road was Jay Shanahan. Jay was the pub's "Fear a'Tí" or "man of the house." He was so passionate about the origins of all the elements that make up the pub that he created the "Jay Walk" to help describe them to customers. Here is how he tells the tale of Raglan Road.

Before We Begin

Everything in the pub has been imported, lock, stock and barrel, from Ireland, except for the toilets. They came from Kohler in Milwaukee, Wisconsin. The panels in the Raglan Snug and the Raglan Room, for instance, are more than 180 years old, and some of the furniture is quite valuable.

The Raglan Room

The original Raglan Road is found in an exclusive part of Dublin where you will also find the U.S. Embassy, so the accent in the Raglan Room is on luxury and refinement. Two high armchairs, a fireplace and Georgian furniture add elegance; some timber panels that came from refurbished houses on Raglan Road itself add authenticity. There are two false doors in the panels – one on the right of the fireplace and the other to the left of the mural of Patrick Kavanagh and Luke Kelly.

The Restroom Corridor

The rest rooms are identified by their Irish titles "Fir" and "Mna." Fir is the Gaelic word for men. Mna, pronounced "minaw," is Gaelic for women.

Once you've figured out which door to open, you can relax and enjoy a photo collection along the corridor that may test your knowledge of contemporary Irish music and celebrity.

The Main Room

As you exit the corridor to the restrooms, you will see the "Mona Lisa" drinking her pint. But look across at the pillar on your right. The man in the photo is playing a "bodhran" (pronounced bow-rawn – as in "take a bow, Ron"). The bodhran is a traditional Irish instrument made from animal hide stretched over a circular piece of timber at high heat, then nailed down with tacks. The facing side of the bodhran is often painted with Celtic designs.

On the far side of the stage you can see a portrait of Bono on the wall backing onto the kitchen exit. Then look at the photos on the right – especially the lowest one. These are "uileann" pipes (pronounced ill-in.) They might look like Scottish bagpipes, but they have no mouthpiece through which to blow. Instead, they are inflated by the arms of the musician who has a cord strapped to his arm attached to a bellows. When he raises his arm, the bellows inflates and the sound is similar to that of bagpipes and just as pleasing.

Now gaze toward the ceiling of the main bar. A series of faces at the top of the pillars are characteristic of the Georgian architecture that can be found throughout Dublin.

Ireland was part of the British Empire before winning independence in 1922, and Dublin was considered the second city of the Empire, which explains the abundance of fine architecture throughout the city.

The dancer's stage in the center of the room was formerly a preacher's pulpit. Like the furniture, this too was imported from Ireland and has now been put to a more entertaining use.

Around the corner, the "High Falutin" Snug is decorated with photos of everyday life in Dublin.

Paddy's Bar

Paddy's Bar has several intriguing features. The series of drawers that you see here were actually made from an old apothecary, or chemist's shop, in Ireland and are at least 160 years old. On the handles of the drawers are the names of original lotions and potions used to cure all ills.

The traditional Irish pub would also double as the village grocery and retail store. Some of these drawers might contain everything from shoelaces to combs to bags of loose-leaf tea. Now look at the shelves on the back wall. The panels include everything from a pewter teapot to a ceramic hot water bottle.

The Music Room

The music room contains two portraits, many photos and a collection of bric-a-brac synonymous with Irish traditional music. One features Bob Geldof, who shot to fame in the 1980s with his punk rock band, the Boomtown Rats. Geldof is also known for helping to make the 1984 "Live Aid" concert, which raised global awareness of famine and the AIDS virus in Africa, a reality.

The photo collection also showcases traditional Irish "Ceili" (pronounced kay-lee) dancing. The Ceili is a group or community dance in the fashion of a square dance, though quite different. If you look at the top photo of the pillar near Paddy's Bar, you'll see the image of a man sitting at a table with a fiddle under his chin. Before him are his pint and his paper and behind him is a group of people who can only find a seat on the stairway. This is a classic traditional Irish music session.

The displays on the far side of the Music Room contain items that are up to a century old. There's a phonograph for playing vinyl records, a Seltzer, a Hohner accordion, a fiddle and a variety of music manuscripts that pre-date the Second World War.

The Library Bar

In the Library, there are two portraits, more photos and other bric-a-brac. A portrait of James Joyce is essential, as he's regarded as Ireland's greatest writer. Joyce's greatest works include "Ulysses," "Finnegan's Wake," and "A Portrait of the Artist as a Young Man." Despite his fame, Joyce's works can be slow going and are not widely read by the general public in Ireland.

Irish playwright Sean O'Casey also gets a spot on the Library Bar wall. His most well-known plays include "The Plough and the Stars," "Shadow of a Gunman," and "Juno and the Paycock."

If you look at the glass display unit, you will see, among other items, a book of plays by George Bernard Shaw. There are also deeds to a property in Dublin dating back to 1776 – the same year that the American Constitution was signed. When you visit the pub, see if you can find it.

The Main Bar

The Main Bar is modeled on old Victorian pubs in Dublin. The small stamp-like tiles were all placed there individually in the original bar. Other features include the marble-top counter and the black, amber and red tiles on the floor that are characteristic of 19th century Dublin architecture.

Having wandered around Raglan Road in the company of the charming Jay Shanahan, we now travel north from Florida to Boston, Mass., to see how one American Irish family ensures that the fish served in the pub meet the high standards of chef Kevin Dundon.

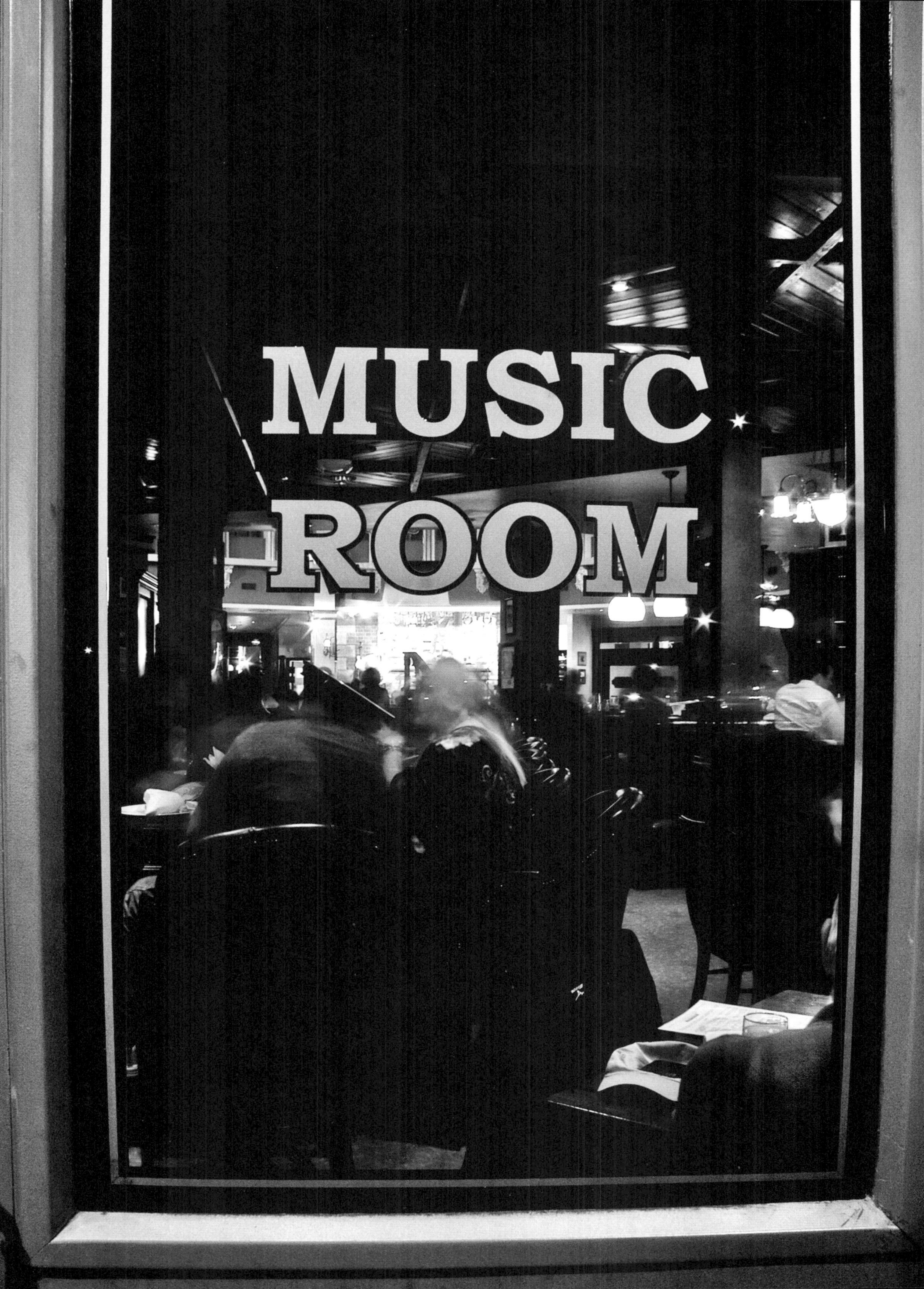
MUSIC
ROOM

Cold Desserts

Recipes for savoury dishes come into fashion and sometimes disappear, but traditional cold desserts seem to have a lot more staying power. Dishes like Classic Sherry Trifle, Strawberry Pavlova and Traditional Deep Filled Apple Pie never seem to lose their appeal. These, like the hot desserts, are also dishes that my mother and grandmother served up back in Ireland, so tucking into them is literally like getting a taste of my childhood.

Others like the Dunbrody Chocolate Jaffa Kiss are dishes that I've invented based around a particular childhood experience (in this case the taste of Jaffa Cake biscuits). More sophisticated dishes like the Chocolate & Orange Tart and the Pear Bakewell Tart also have their links back to Ireland.

SERVES 8-10

Chocolate & Orange Tart

Chocolate is one of my favourite ingredients for baking. This tart can be quite an impressive dinner party option, or you could just quietly enjoy it with a cup of tea or coffee when nobody else is around to judge you!

INGREDIENTS

Chocolate ganache
125ml/4fl oz/generous
½ cup cream
60ml/2fl oz/generous
⅜ cup milk
75g/2¾oz/2¾ squares
dark chocolate
75g/2¾oz/2¾ squares
milk chocolate
1 egg

Sweet pastry
55g/2oz/¼ cup butter
55g/2oz/¼ cup superfine sugar
125g/4½oz/generous ½ cup,
firmly packed plain flour
1 egg

Candied orange
2 oranges, zest and juice
55g/2oz/¼ cup sugar

METHOD

To prepare the sweet pastry
Cream the butter and sugar together, then add the sifted flour. Stir in the beaten egg and, using a knife, combine the ingredients together. Wrap in cling film and refrigerate for at least 2 hours.

Grease a 23cm/9-inch fluted pie dish. Roll out the pastry on a lightly floured surface. Roll the pastry onto the rolling pin and line over the pie dish. Pre-bake at 180°C/350°F for 20 minutes.

Candied orange
Remove the zest from the orange and cut into thin strips. Blanch the zest for 2 minutes in some boiling water. Drain and set aside to cool. Repeat the operation again, using clean water each time, to get rid of the bitterness.

Make a sugar syrup using the sugar and 2 tablespoons water. Add the orange zest to the syrup and allow to cook over a low

heat for about 30 minutes. Remove from the heat and allow the orange to cool and dry for a few hours.

Ganache
Bring the cream and milk to the boil and add the chocolate pieces. Whisk together to obtain a smooth cream-like consistency. Whisk the egg in a small bowl before adding to the creamy chocolate mixture. The mixture should ideally be at around 35°C/95°F.

Assembling the tart
Arrange the candied orange at the bottom on the base of the cooked pastry. Pour the chocolate ganache over the orange and pastry and bake in the oven at 180°C/350°F/Gas Mark 4 for 10 minutes.

Allow to cool, then refrigerate. Remove from the fridge at least 10 minutes before serving.

SERVES 4

Dundons Delight

This is a light and refreshing dessert perfect for long, warm summer days.

INGREDIENTS

Pavlova
4 egg whites
225g/8oz/1 cup superfine sugar
½ tsp cornflour
½ tsp vanilla essence
½ tsp white wine vinegar

Consommé
225g/8oz strawberries
115g/4oz/½ cup superfine sugar
1 glass (150ml/5fl oz/⅔ cup)
champagne or sparkling wine
juice of ½ lemon

METHOD

Preheat oven to 110°C/225°F/ Gas Mark ½. Put the egg whites into the spotlessly clean mixing bowl of a stand mixer and beat on full speed until they're quite stiff. Turn the speed of the mixer down and slowly add the sugar, pouring in just a little at a time. When all the sugar has gone in, add the vanilla essence, cornflour and white wine vinegar and give one final whisk on high speed.

When ready, the mixture should be glossy and if you turn the bowl upside down the mixture should remain in the bowl. Go on, try it!

Meanwhile prepare your tin. Line an oblong baking tray, 33 x 23cm/13 x 9 inches, with parchment paper. Using two tablespoons, mould the meringue into quenelles and place them carefully on the prepared baking trays.

Bake in the oven for 1 hour until the meringue mixture is very firm to touch but still soft in the middle. I normally leave mine to cool down in the oven with the heat off and the door open.

Meanwhile make up the strawberry consommé. Put the strawberries, sugar, champagne and lemon juice in a large bowl and set it over a saucepan of simmering water. Cook for 10-12 minutes or until all of the strawberries have softened down and you've got a sauce.

To serve, pour a little of the consommé into a large bowl, sit the pavlova on top of the consommé and arrange a scoop of vanilla ice cream either beside or under the pavlova.

Garnish with additional strawberries.

SERVES 6

Dunbrody Chocolate Jaffa Kiss

Chocolate and oranges go together very well and although there is quite a bit of preparation involved in making this dish the end result is well worth it!

INGREDIENTS

450g/1lb milk and dark chocolate, broken into pieces
4 eggs, separated
500ml/17fl oz/generous 2 cups cream
300g/10oz/scant ⅞ cup marmalade

Sponge
4 eggs
115g/4oz/½ cup superfine sugar
115g/4oz/1 cup, firmly packed self-raising flour

Ganache
150g/5½oz/5½ squares dark chocolate
250ml/9fl oz/scant 1¼ cups cream, plus a little extra if necessary
a handful of strawberries and raspberries, halved, to decorate

Chocolate shards
200g/7oz dark chocolate
50g/1¾oz/1¾ squares white chocolate

METHOD

Marmalade
Spoon some marmalade into ice cube tray and leave to set in the freezer for a minimum of 4 hours but preferably overnight.

Sponge
Preheat the oven to 180°C/350°F/ Gas Mark 4. Grease and line an oblong 33x 23cm/13 x 9 inch tin with parchment paper.

In a mixing bowl, beat the eggs with the sugar for the sponge base. It should become very light and aerated. The whisk should leave a figure of eight on the surface of the mixture when lifted out of it.

Gently fold in the sifted flour with a metal spoon. Be very gentle so as not to knock any of the generated air out of the sponge base but, at the same time, make sure that all of the flour is incorporated. Pour the mixture into a prepared tin.

Bake for 20 minutes until well-risen and golden brown. Take the sponge out of the oven and leave to cool down on a rack. When cooled, cut for the base of the kiss using a pastry cutter.

Chocolate mousse
Melt the milk and dark chocolate in a heatproof bowl set over a pan of simmering water. Leave to cool a little. Lightly beat the egg yolks and then whisk them into the melted chocolate until well combined. Whip the cream in a bowl until you have soft peaks and then whisk the cream into the chocolate mixture.

In a separate bowl, beat the egg whites until stiff and then fold into the chocolate mixture. Divide among the moulds of your choice, and insert the frozen cube of marmalade into the centre, finishing by adding the circle of sponge on top.

Chocolate ganache

Place the chocolate and cream in a pan and cook gently for 4-5 minutes until melted, stirring continuously. The consistency should coat the back of a wooden spoon. If you think it's too thick, add a little more cream. Use immediately or transfer to a bowl, cover with cling film and chill until needed. This will keep happily for two days in the fridge and unhappily thereafter.

When almost ready to serve, warm the chocolate ganache in a heatproof bowl set over a pan of simmering water. Invert the frozen mousse onto a wire rack set over a clean tray and then carefully peel away the mould. Ladle a little of the chocolate ganache over each one until completely coated, allowing the excess to drip on to the tray below. Using a spatula, scrape the excess chocolate ganache into a small pan.

Allow to defrost and decorate with the strawberries and raspberries and drizzle around the cooled chocolate ganache.

Chocolate shards

Now to make the chocolate shards. Melt the dark chocolate in a heatproof bowl set over a pan of simmering water. Repeat with the white chocolate in a separate bowl. Leave to cool to room temperature.

Line a baking sheet with cling film. Spoon on blobs of the dark and white chocolate and then cover with another piece of cling film. Gently roll until the chocolate blobs meet and form one even layer. Place in the freezer for at least 10 minutes or up to one month.

Working quickly, remove the sheet of chocolate from the freezer and peel away the cling film, then break into shards and stick two into the top of each Dunbrody Kiss.

Kevin's tip

Silicone moulds are best but you could use teacups or ramekins lined with cling film. Place in the freezer for at least 2 hours.

TEA: THIRSTY HABIT 'IRELAND'S EVIL?'

When people hear the word "tea," they tend to think of the drink as an English obsession. But, in fact, the Irish drink more black tea per head than anywhere else in the world, with some thirsty Irish folks consuming up to 10 cups every day. If the English are obsessed, then the Irish are fanatical about the beverage.

The tea-drinking habit really took hold in Ireland from about the 1830s onward. Wealthier, land-owning classes were always able to pay the high price of tea leaves that were transported from India and China to Britain, then imported to Ireland. But in the middle of the 1800s, the price of tea fell dramatically and what had once been a luxury became affordable for most everyone.

The quality of this influx of cheap tea was poor, however, so ordinary Irish people brewed it strongly and added milk to improve the taste. This preference for strong tea remains today and explains why you might hear Irish people say with pride that the tea was "so strong you could trot a mouse on it" or "so strong it stirred itself."

A slow poison

Tea became so popular in Ireland that, in April 1910, the New York Times special correspondent in London quoted an inspector of Irish national schools, under the title "Tea is Ireland's Evil," saying:

" . . . The use of tea is now carried to such dangerous excess that it ranks before alcohol as an enemy of the public health." He also claimed that tea has "the properties of a slow poison." Despite such scaremongering, Ireland's love of tea continued. The Pioneer Total Abstinence Association, formed in 1898 in Dublin, promoted tea in place of alcohol and further drove sales.

After the Second World War, Ireland began to import its own tea direct from China, Africa and India instead of from British auction houses. And Irish tea companies began creating their own blends. But it's still the strongest teas like "Breakfast Blend" that are preferred for their high caffeine levels and consumed at all times of the day.

"Other people have a
nationality. The Irish
and the Jews have
a psychosis."

Brendan Behan (Irish playwright)

SERVES 4-6

Pear Bakewell Tart

An impressive summer dessert which is delicious with mascarpone or your favourite ice cream.

INGREDIENTS

6-8 pears, peeled and halved
450g/1lb shortcrust pastry
115g/4oz/½ cup
butter, softened
115g/4oz/1 cup icing sugar
115g/4oz/scant 1 cup
ground almonds
25g/1oz/scant ¼ cup cornflour
2 large eggs
55g/2oz/½ cup flaked almonds
1 tbsp apricot jam, to glaze
2 tbsp water

For the poaching syrup
900ml/1½ pint/4 cups water
200g/7oz/1¾ cups
superfine sugar
1 lemon, sliced into wedges
1 star anise, optional

METHOD

Using a rolling pin, roll out the pastry on a lightly floured surface. Prepare a 20cm/8-inch tart tin by lightly greasing it and place the pastry on top. Press the pastry into the edges and trim.

Prepare the pears by peeling them and removing the seeds then slice each pear in half. In a large saucepan, add the water, superfine sugar, lemon and star anise. Bring the mixture to the boil, then reduce the heat to a simmer and add the pears to poach them. Cook for 10-12 minutes until the pears have softened then remove the pears from the syrup and allow to cool.

To make the frangipane, place the butter, sugar, almonds, cornflour and eggs into a bowl and whisk until the mixture has a smooth consistency. Pour the mixture over the pastry, and place the halved pears on top. Sprinkle with the flaked almonds. Place in a preheated oven at 180°C/350°F/ Gas Mark 4 for 30-40 minutes until golden brown on top.

To make the glaze, mix the apricot jam with water and heat over a moderate heat until the jam has dissolved.

Remove the bakewell tart from the oven and glaze immediately.

MORE 'CAM-A-LITTLE' THAN 'CAMELOT'

Let's be honest about this – there's no castle any longer. If you come to Dublin expecting to see a deep moat, stone towers and mighty fortifications; you know, the sort of place from which knights of old might have ridden forth, you might be disappointed.

Dublin Castle does, however, comprise a kind of condensed history of Ireland.

Dublin Garden, which lies just behind the castle, is the site of the original "black pool" or "Dubh Linn" that gave Dublin its name when founded by the Vikings following their invasion in the 9th century A.D. There's also the Norman Record Tower, the sole remaining part of the castle built in 1204 by King John following the Norman invasion of Ireland. King John, perhaps best remembered as the king in the "Robin Hood" legend, built a series of castles across the country to secure Ireland for the Normans who had invaded and held neighbouring Britain since 1066 AD. Many attempts were made to lay seige to the castle and take it, but all failed.

"I spent a lot of money on booze, birds and fast cars. The rest I just squandered."

George Best (Northern Irish soccer player)

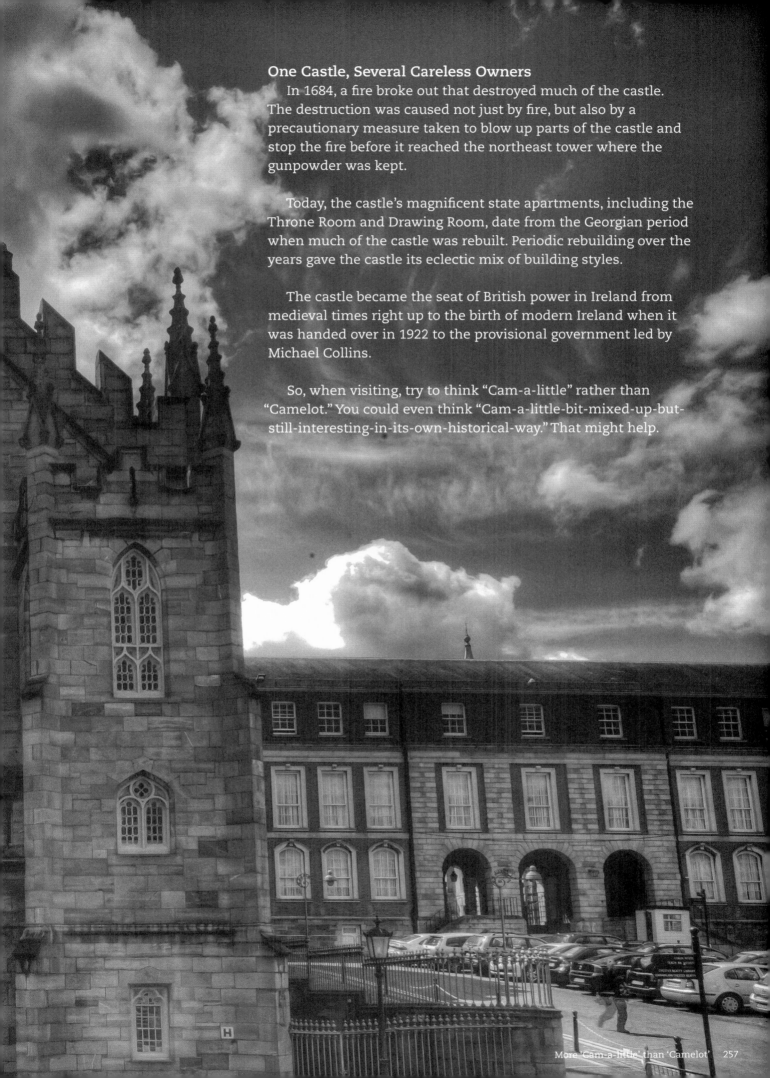

One Castle, Several Careless Owners

In 1684, a fire broke out that destroyed much of the castle. The destruction was caused not just by fire, but also by a precautionary measure taken to blow up parts of the castle and stop the fire before it reached the northeast tower where the gunpowder was kept.

Today, the castle's magnificent state apartments, including the Throne Room and Drawing Room, date from the Georgian period when much of the castle was rebuilt. Periodic rebuilding over the years gave the castle its eclectic mix of building styles.

The castle became the seat of British power in Ireland from medieval times right up to the birth of modern Ireland when it was handed over in 1922 to the provisional government led by Michael Collins.

So, when visiting, try to think "Cam-a-little" rather than "Camelot." You could even think "Cam-a-little-bit-mixed-up-but-still-interesting-in-its-own-historical-way." That might help.

SERVES 4

Classic Sherry Trifle

Sherry trifle is one of those desserts that has been around forever and will never be far from our tables. Everybody has his or her own take on it but what few people know is that the classic sherry trifle does not contain jelly. Revolutionary, eh! Here is my twist on this classic and well-loved dessert.

INGREDIENTS

Jam Swiss roll
4 eggs
115g/4oz/½ cup sugar
115g/4oz/1 cup
self-raising flour

Fresh egg custard
450ml/¾ pint/scant
2 cups milk
150ml/5fl oz/⅔ cup cream
½ vanilla pod
6 egg yolks
85g/3oz/generous
⅓ cup sugar
2 tsp cornflour

Garnish
4 dessertspoons fresh
raspberry jam
225g/8oz fresh berries such
as raspberries, strawberries,
blackcurrants etc
55g/2oz/¼ cup superfine sugar
100ml/3½fl oz/scant ½ cup
sherry, good quality
250ml/9fl oz/scant 1¼ cups
freshly whipped cream
55g/2oz flaked almonds

METHOD

Jam Swiss roll
Preheat the oven to 180°C/350°F/ Gas Mark 4. Grease and line an oblong, 33 x 23cm/13 x 9 inch, tin with parchment paper.

In a mixing bowl, beat the 4 eggs with the sugar for the sponge base. It should become very light and aerated. The whisk should leave a figure of eight on the surface of the mixture when the whisk is lifted out of it.

Gently fold in the sifted flour with a metal spoon. Be very gentle so as not to knock any of the generated air out of the sponge base but at the same time, make sure that all of the flour is incorporated.

Pour the mixture into a prepared Swiss roll tin. Bake for 20 minutes, until well-risen and golden brown. Take the sponge out of the oven.

Before the sponge is fully cooled, invert it onto a sheet of parchment paper dusted with 55g/2oz of the superfine sugar and spread with a thin layer of raspberry jam. Carefully roll the Swiss roll up, starting from the longest side.

When rolled up, slice into thin slices and arrange in individual glasses or a large bowl, making sure that the bottom of the glass or bowl is lined all the way around. Retain a little of the sponge for the middle if you want. Sprinkle with some freshly cut fruit, additional jam if you like, and a generous helping of sherry. If you like a lot of sponge, you can put in more than one layer.

Custard
Split the vanilla pod lengthways and with a small sharp knife scrape out the seeds of one half of the pod. Put the seeds and the half pod into the milk and cream in a large saucepan. Wrap the remainder of the vanilla pod and retain for later use. Bring the milk, cream and vanilla pod to the boil.

Meanwhile in a large spotlessly clean bowl, use a whisk to beat the egg yolks, sugar and cornflour together until light and creamy. Spend about 2 minutes on this process. Pour the boiled milk and cream mixture onto the eggs and mix well.

Return the mixture to the saucepan and cook until the mixture coats the back of a wooden spoon. It is important to stir the mixture at all times to prevent it from curdling. This process should take no more than 2 minutes on a very gentle heat. Do not allow the mixture to boil. Taste the custard to make sure that you cannot taste the cornflour. If you can, return to the heat and stir continuously on a low heat for another minute or so.

Pour the custard over the sponge mixture and allow to cool for a couple of hours or overnight.

Cover with a disc of parchment paper or cling film to prevent the formation of a crust on top of the custard.

Pipe some whipped cream on the top and sprinkle with some flaked and toasted almonds. Alternatively, you can arrange with fresh fruit.

Kevin's tip
If you wish you can put a spoon or two of sherry into the custard for an increased flavour.

Rhubarb Pannacotta

This deliciously light and creamy dessert is simple to make. Try it on its own sprinkled with hazelnuts or with a mix of sharp fresh summer berries.

INGREDIENTS

50g/1¾oz/scant ¼
cup superfine sugar
juice of ½ orange
2 tbsp Cointreau or
orange liqueur
400ml/14fl oz/1¾ cups cream
100g/3½oz/½ cup
superfine sugar
½ vanilla pod
2 leaves of gelatine soaked
in water for 5 minutes

METHOD

Fruit base

Place the rhubarb and sugar into a small saucepan over a medium heat and pour over the orange juice. Cook for 4-5 minutes until the sugar has dissolved then, tilting the pan on its side, add the liqueur and set it alight. When the flames have died down, remove the pan from the heat and divide the rhubarb mixture between four serving glasses. Set aside and allow to cool.

Pannacotta

Put the cream and sugar and vanilla into a pot and bring slowly to the boil. Take the leaves of gelatine and put them into a bowl of cold water to soften. Strain the gelatine with a fine sieve to remove any excess moisture. Take the cream off the heat and whisk in the gelatine. Allow to chill slightly before pouring over the rhubarb.

Kevin's tip

When pouring over the fruit, pour the unset pannacotta over the back of a teaspoon to ensure you don't disturb the rhubarb compote in the glass.

SERVES 6

Banoffi Pie

With a thick layer of biscuits, smothered in golden caramel, topped with sliced bananas and freshly whipped cream, what's not to love about this banoffi pie recipe!

INGREDIENTS

Biscuit base
550g/1¼lb digestive biscuits
250g/9oz butter

Topping
2 cans (2 x 400g/14oz) condensed milk
6 large bananas
350ml/12fl oz/1½ cups cream
50g/1¼oz/1¼ squares chocolate, melted
200ml/7fl oz/generous ¾ cup whipped cream, to serve

METHOD

Biscuit base
Using either a food processor or a plastic bag and a rolling pin, crush the biscuits into small pieces. Do not make them too fine, as it's nice to leave a little bit of crunch in the base.

Melt the butter and add it into the biscuits to bind them together. The mixture should not be too wet at this stage.

Press this mixture into a 25cm/10-inch cheesecake springform tin and place into the fridge to set for a few minutes whilst you make up the topping.

Topping
The condensed milk needs to be prepared the day before to allow it to cool down.

NOTE
Extreme caution must be taken during this process. Place the tins of condensed milk into a large saucepan and fully cover with water. It's very important to ensure that they are always covered with water, so add water to the pan when needed to make sure the pan never boils dry. Bring the water to the boil, then reduce the heat and allow to simmer for approximately 3 hours. Remove from the heat and allow the cans of condensed milk to cool in the water, preferably overnight.

When cool, open the cans of condensed milk and spread the caramel over the prepared biscuit base in a lovely thick layer.

Peel and slice the bananas and place a layer of them on top of the caramel. Add the whipped cream, then drizzle with the melted chocolate.

Transfer the entire dessert to the fridge for at least one hour to set. Remove from the tin and transfer onto a serving platter. Decorate with fresh berries.

SERVES 12 CUP CAKES

Chocolate Topped Cup Cakes

These cupcakes make for a perfect treat for any occasion. I love baking them for a child's birthday party or simply to munch with a cup of tea in the late morning, afternoon or evening (alright, they taste good at any time of the day or night and why should the kids have all the fun?).

INGREDIENTS

200g/7oz/⅞ cup butter
200g/7oz/⅞ cup superfine sugar
1 tsp vanilla extract
5 large eggs
400g/14oz/3½ cups, firmly packed plain flour
1 tsp baking powder

Topping
200g/7oz/⅞ cup butter
400g/14oz/4 cups icing sugar
55g/2oz chocolate sauce

Chocolate shards
200g/7oz/7 squares plain chocolate
50g/1¾oz/1¾ squares white chocolate

METHOD

Preheat the oven to 350F/180C/Gas Mark 4. To make the cupcakes, soften the butter and beat in a large mixing bowl with the sugar. Add in the vanilla extract at this stage also and beat well until the mixture is really light and fluffy.

When this mixture is creamy and fluffy add in the eggs and sieve in the flour. If you find the mixture is a little tight you can add a dessertspoon of milk to loosen it up a little.

Line a 12-cup muffin tray with deep muffin papers. Divide the mixture between the muffin papers, filling about halfway full.

Bake for 20-25 minutes until well risen and cooked through and then allow to cool.

When the cupcakes are cool you can make up the topping. Using an electric hand whisker beat the butter until smooth and creamy. Gradually add the icing sugar and beat until creamy and well combined with the butter. Pour in the chocolate and spoon through once or twice to create a marbled effect.

To serve, use a piping bag to pipe the topping onto the cupcakes or spread it over the top using the back of a spoon.

To make the chocolate shards
Melt the plain chocolate in a heatproof bowl set over a pan of simmering water. Repeat with the white chocolate in a separate bowl. Leave to cool to room temperature. Line a baking sheet with cling film. Spoon on blobs of the plain and white chocolate and then cover with another piece of cling film. Gently roll so that the chocolate blobs meet and form one even layer. Place in the freezer for at least 10 minutes (they're good for up to one month in there). Remove from the freezer, roughly break the chocolate into shards and add pieces to the topping on the cupcakes.

I KNOW WHAT YOU DID 365 MILLION SUMMERS AGO

Ireland is renowned for its ancient sites and monuments.

The oldest footprints in Europe and, indeed, the whole of the world's northern hemisphere are found on rocks in Valentia Island off the coast of County Kerry in Ireland. About 200 fossilized footprints of primitive vertebrates discovered only a few decades ago are estimated to be from 365 to 385 million years old.

To put that in perspective, scientists believe that dinosaurs did not appear on earth until 150 million years after these footprints were made. The tracks appear to have been formed when a four-legged amphibian about three feet long walked over mud flats close to a shoreline. The tracks were eventually covered by silt and, over thousands of years, the mud below formed into slate rock, preserving the parallel footprints that run for roughly 50 feet. You can clearly see a depression between the sets of footprints that may have been caused by the primitive amphibian dragging its tail behind it. But, really, we're only guessing.

Dr. Matthew Parkes of the Geological Survey of Ireland explains: "The footprints are very important because they mark the transition for vertebrates, which had been living in water. They came out to live on land and developed limbs and breathed air."

Similar footprints have been discovered in other parts of the world, including Australia, but it's interesting to note that Ireland has been welcoming visitors to its shores since before the days of the dinosaurs.

"Always forgive your enemies, nothing annoys them as much."

Oscar Wilde (Irish playwright)

SERVES 6

Traditional Deep Filled Apple Pie

What could be more American than apple pie? Well, I might as well break it to you that other nations love this dish just as much (and some might have been around even longer than the USA). Whether it's served with freshly whipped cream or homemade custard this is a favourite homemade treat all over the world.

INGREDIENTS

Shortcrust pastry
350g/12oz/3 cups, firmly packed plain flour
pinch of salt
175g/6oz/¾ cup hard butter
1 level tbsp sugar
ice cold water, approximately 60–80ml/2–2¾fl oz/generous ¼–⅓ cup

Filling
4-5 cooking apples
85g/3oz/generous ⅓ cup superfine sugar
¼ tsp ground cinnamon

Glaze
1 egg
100ml/3½fl oz/scant ½ cup milk

METHOD

Begin by making the pastry. Sift the flour into a large mixing bowl. Add in the pinch of salt. Cut the butter into cubes and add this to the flour and salt. Using the tips of your fingers rub the butter into the flour until the mixture resembles fine breadcrumbs.

Add in the sugar. Next add the water, little by little, until the mixture all comes together into a ball. Knead lightly to achieve a smooth pastry and then wrap it in cling film and refrigerate for about 1 hour.

Preheat the oven to 160°C/325°F/ Gas Mark 3. Roll the pastry out to line a quiche dish or a large plate, approximately 23–25cm/9-10 inches in diameter.

In a separate bowl mix the sliced apples, sugar and cinnamon together. Pour the apple mixture onto the pastry, ensuring an even spread on the base. Place the upper layer of pastry on top of the apple mixture, sealing the sides tightly together with either a knife or a fork.

Make up the egg wash glaze by whisking together the egg and milk. Brush the egg wash over the top pastry and make one or two little vents in it with a sharp knife.

Bake the pie for approximately 40-45 minutes until the pastry is golden brown and when removed from the oven sprinkle with a little superfine sugar. Serve with your favourite ice cream or custard, or lashings of fresh cream.

Kevin's tip
This pie recipe works equally well with rhubarb or gooseberries, just leave out the cinnamon.

Strawberry Pavlova

Use any variation of fresh summer berries such as raspberries, blueberries, loganberries or blackberries.

INGREDIENTS

Pavlova
6 egg whites
350g/12oz/1½ cups
superfine sugar
½ tsp vanilla essence
½ tsp cornflour
½ tsp white wine vinegar

Garnish
250ml/9fl oz/scant 1¼ cups
cream, very softly whipped
16-20 Wexford strawberries,
cut into quarters

METHOD

Preheat oven to 120°C/250°F/Gas Mark ½. Put the egg whites into a spotlessly clean mixing bowl of a stand mixer and beat on full speed until they're quite stiffly beaten. Turn the speed of the mixer down and slowly add the sugar a little at a time. When all the sugar has been mixed in, add the vanilla essence, cornflour and vinegar and give one final whisk on high speed.

When ready, the mixture should be glossy and when the bowl is turned upside down the mixture should remain stationary in the bowl. Yes, really. Want to try it?

Meanwhile prepare your tin. Line an oblong baking tray, 33 x 23cm/13 x 9 inches, with parchment paper. You can either spread all the mixture out on the baking sheet or, using a piping bag, you can pipe the mixture out into attractive individual shapes of your own design.

Bake in the oven for 1 hour until the meringue mixture is very firm to touch but still soft in the middle. I normally leave mine to cool in the oven with the heat off and the door open.

When the Pavlova base is cold, transfer to a serving platter and spoon over the softly whipped cream. Add the strawberry quarters on top of the cream. Serve immediately!

Kevin's tip
If you somehow manage to resist serving this dish immediately and, instead, make it early to serve it later, don't place the cream or strawberries on top of the meringue base, as they will soak into it, making it a bit soggy and ruining the crisp exterior that everyone loves.

SERVES 4

Knickerbocker Glory

Traditionally served in a long glass, Knickerbocker Glory brings back memories of my childhood when I would request it on visits to restaurants and devour every last mouthful. This is a more contemporary version to tantalise your tastebuds.

INGREDIENTS

Raspberry jelly
55g/2oz/¼ cup superfine sugar
50ml/1¾fl oz/scant ¼ cup water
½ lemon juice
4 leaves gelatine leaf, soaked
400ml/14fl oz/1¾ cups raspberry juice,
1 punnet (250g/9oz) strawberries
1 punnet (100g/3½oz) blueberries
1 punnet (200g/7oz) raspberries

Raspberry coulis
100g/3½ oz raspberries
scant 25g/1oz/¼ cup icing sugar
juice of ½ lemon

Vanilla mousse
250g/9oz/generous 1 cup mascarpone
10oz/300g cream, lightly whipped
1 vanilla pod

To serve
4 scoops strawberry ice cream
4-8 macaroons
1 bar of chocolate, grated

METHOD

Place the sugar, water, lemon juice and 200ml/7fl oz/generous ¾ cup of the raspberry juice in a saucepan over a moderate heat. When the sugar has fully dissolved, remove from the heat and add in the gelatine, stir until fully disintegrated into the liquid. Now stir in the remaining raspberry juice.

Prepare the serving glass by placing some fresh berries into the base of the glass, pour over some of the jelly. Place in the fridge for 40 minutes. Add the remaining jelly, being careful not to fill the glasses more than three-quarters full. Return to the fridge for an extra 2 hours.

In the meantime, prepare the vanilla mousse by placing the mascarpone, cream and seeds from the vanilla pod into a large mixing bowl and combine all the ingredients together until soft peaks are formed. Store in the fridge until required.

To make the coulis, blitz the raspberries in a food processor with the icing sugar and the lemon. Pass through a fine sieve.

To serve, place some fresh fruit berries onto the set jelly and top with 1 scoop of vanilla mousse, 1 scoop of strawberry ice cream and a drizzle of raspberry coulis. Finish off with a macaroon or two and some grated chocolate.

Homemade Chocolate Chip Cookies

These cookies keep perfectly for up to 4-5 days if stored in an airtight container, but more often than not they don't get stored and are eaten warm. All of them!

INGREDIENTS

115g/4oz/½ cup butter
85g/3oz/generous ⅓ cup, firmly
packed brown sugar
70g/2½oz/scant ⅓ cup,
firmly packed superfine sugar
1 egg
1 tsp vanilla extract
2 tbsp honey
1 pinch salt
250g/9oz/2¼ cups,
firmly packed flour
1 tsp baking powder
200g/7oz mixed chocolate chips,
or a good-quality bar, roughly
chopped and minus the bits
you just have to taste to test
the chocolate!

METHOD

Preheat the oven to 160°C/325°F/Gas Mark 3. In a bowl, cream together the butter, brown sugar and superfine sugar until the sugar has fully dissolved and you've got a smooth and creamy cookie batter. Add the eggs, vanilla extract, honey and salt, and mix well for a further minute.

Sift in the flour and baking powder and combine using a wooden spoon. Sprinkle over the chocolate chips and ensure they are well mixed through.

Using a spoon or your hands, make small balls of cookie dough about 2cm/1 inch size, and place on a parchment-lined baking tray.

Dip the tines of a fork in some water and push lightly on the cookies to flatten them. Place in the preheated oven for 7-10 minutes until golden.

Remove from the oven and allow to cool before serving. Store in an airtight container if you're particularly strong-willed.

A VERY PECULIAR PINT

If you've ever been inside a pub and ordered a pint of Guinness, you may have noticed a strange phenomenon that has nothing whatsoever to do with the effects of alcohol. At least that's what we believe.

Of course, the pouring of a pint of Guinness is itself a bit of a protracted business. The barman starts pouring the dark stuff into the glass and then, when it's only about two- thirds full, he places it on the counter and seems to lose interest. Many people have become irate at this point, mistakenly thinking that he has forgotten all about their half-poured drink, but he's merely waiting for it to settle. After a minute or two, he will stroll over and "whisper" the remains of the pint into the glass. Now it's yours to savour.

When you look into your glass, you see what appears to be a time-lapse sequence of all the wet summer holidays of your childhood. Don't be tempted to sip just yet. The Guinness is settling itself down again and while it does you might notice the phenomenon of the cascade.

All in the Cause of Science

It's the bubbles. They're going downward, not up. It's not magic; it's science. A central column of the Guinness rises faster than the liquid at the sides, creating a current that drags the liquid nearest the glass downward. Dr Andrew Alexander of Edinburgh University's School of Chemistry has studied the effect in detail:

"Our group carried out preliminary experiments at a local pub a few years ago, but the results proved inconclusive," he says. "But now we have produced video proof that the bubbles do actually go down the inside of the glass."

Notice that Dr Alexander uses the phrase "proved inconclusive." Like all good scientists, he was wise enough to extend the research phase so that more Guinness could be sampled to test the effect. It's truly amazing what dedicated people will do to further the cause of science.

"Work like you don't need the money, love like you've never been hurt, and dance like no one is watching."

Bono (Irish musician)

Take three

Raglan Road is very passionate about the ingredients we use in our kitchens every day. We make all of our dishes from scratch, fresh every day. And that is what makes Raglan so popular. Guests can taste the difference in our food. So we go to great lengths to source the very finest ingredients we can find from local and national suppliers. And when we friend a great ingredients supplier we celebrate them. So here are just three of our partners in food. People and companies who go to remarkable lengths to deliver us with great food ingredients – every day.

BEST FISHES FROM BOSTON

Faneuil Hall, Dock Square, Boston, Massachusetts, USA.
M.F. Foley: Fishmonger

Michael Frances Foley was the second son at a time when the first son inherited the farm. So he emigrated from County Tipperary, Ireland to Boston, Massachusetts to join a cousin who was already in the fish business there. This was the early 1900s. In Boston, at that time, the Irish were the help. Every morning, Michael, or M.F. as he was known, would call on wealthy Bostonian families in the Back Bay area (using the tradesman's entrance) and, more often than not, the Irishman would find himself talking to the Irish cook who would be responsible for preparing the family meals. This Irish connection worked well then and is still working more than 100 years later. Foley, today, supplies Raglan Road with all their fresh salmon, smoked salmon, mussels, scallops and squid. Chef Kevin Dundon refuses to compromise and insists on preparing fish caught only in the Atlantic, as that is the ocean that surrounds Ireland.

In 1906, M.F. leased space in a flat iron building in Faneuil Hall, and the M.F. Foley Company, selling fish "fresh off the boats," was born. Freshness is still key. Foley buyers are in New England ports every day to examine the fish and ensure they get the last day's catch.

"We buy 'top of the trip' fish. That means fish that are only 24-48 hours out of the water," explains Laura Foley Ramsden, president and co-owner of the M.F. Foley Fish Company. When selecting the highest quality fish, Foley uses the same very strict standards that they've been applying for 106 years.

"Quality fish build customer loyalty for a lifetime," Laura insists. Unlike other distributors, Foley takes orders ahead of time then seeks the best fish to fill them. "We buy it, immediately cut it and send it out the door to our customers so no time is wasted." Foley is still a relatively small company of 80 employees but buys roughly 50,000 pounds of whole fish every day.

"Our buyers do the 'Eyes, Touch, Nose, Temperature' test in the ports." Foley buyers are looking for gills that are bright red (brown gills mean the fish is less fresh) and for bright, clear eyes, another sign of freshness. "In terms of touch," says Laura, "the fish should be stiff. If you put your finger on it and press, you don't want a fingerprint to be left, because soft fish is old fish."

Then it is time to get up close. "We put our noses right into the middle of the fish to smell it, because fresh fish does not smell. If you are smelling something (like an ammonia odor), that something is bacteria." Next, Foley buyers will throw a temperature probe into the fish just to be sure. "In New England, in the summer, a guy on a day boat can go out, and the temperature can go from 60 degrees at the time the fish is caught to 90 degrees very soon after. If fish sits on the deck for several hours at 90 degrees, the whole catch could go bad."

Foley goes to great lengths to ensure that the seafood they source is caught or farmed properly. Laura cites as an example the farmed Blue Hill mussels Foley sources. In some locations, she says, there are so many mussel farms competing for space that the mussels fight for food in the water and, as a result, their meat is smaller. Foley found two farmers in Blue Hill Bay, Maine – the only two mussel farmers there – whose mussels are not competing with large numbers of other mussels and end up much plumper.

Foley also insists on seafood that has not been chemically treated or frozen more than once. They only use domestic Point Judith, Rhode Island squid, whereas a majority of U.S. distributors use a Chinese squid to achieve a lower price point. "The problem is that a lot of those squid have been chemically treated, which destroys some of the flavor, and they are twice-frozen." The Point Judith squid, she says, are not chemically treated and are frozen only once, resulting in sweeter and more tender squid.

"Any time you freeze something, it creates problems with the texture," says Laura. Many outlets in the United States use a Chilean salmon that has been frozen, thawed, smoked, and refrozen. The Foley smoked salmon is fresh Canadian, never-frozen fish, with a "much better, buttery flavour to it."

In the United States, scallopers are able to add chemicals to scallops such as sodium trypolyphosphate. This chemical aids water retention but diminishes the texture and flavour of a natural scallop. To avoid treated scallops, Foley buys their scallops fresh off a boat that has been at sea no more than two days.

"When you eat that scallop at Raglan Road, it will have the natural sweetness and firmness to it with no harsh chemical aftertaste," Laura says.

What happens to the fish after Foley buys it is every bit as important as where it originated. "We're crazy about temperature control," Laura says, "because we know that, for every degree of temperature over 32 F degrees a fish is held, you lose a day of shelf life." Foley makes its own ice with salt added so it has a lower freezing point of 16 F degrees instead of 32 F degrees. The company also ships their fish in metal tins because the metal conducts cold better and fish can be maintained at a constant low temperature. When their fish arrive at Raglan Road, Foley uses a temperature control sensor to guarantee that it has been chilled properly on the journey from Boston to Florida.

Foley runs a School of Fish, an accredited three-day fish seminar that Raglan Road kitchen staffers attend. "We cover everything from hook to skillet," says Laura. Chefs and cooks are taken out on a fishing boat to learn how different types of fish are caught, how fish are handled at sea and how top quality is maintained all the way to the plate of a Raglan Road guest. They also visit the commission houses to examine different gradings of fish, Foley production plants and the fish auctions.

"They eat fish for breakfast, five different fish for lunch and three different fish each night at dinner. We don't let them go until they grow gills," jokes Laura, who has her own favourite fish dish at Raglan Road – the seared smoked salmon with maple butter sauce. "I don't know how they prepare it but, oh my gosh, it is great."

Foley now ships to 38 U.S. states and abroad, but Laura has not visited Tipperary to discover her Irish roots just yet. "I'd love to have time to do it," she says.

One Foley family joke concerns her great-grandmother, who was a Maloney from County Tipperary. The Maloneys were beef farmers, and the joke is that The Foley Company is a beef-fish merger. "We don't like to talk about that," quips Laura. "Beef cattle are the black sheep of our family."

From Boston, we travel 1,400 miles south to Ruskin, Florida, not far from Tampa Bay and the Gulf of Mexico. This time our destination is the land, not the sea.

ROCKET FUEL

3 Boys Farm, Ruskin, Florida, USA.
Robert Tornello: Racing Driver and Hydroponic Farmer

In the 2000-'01 season, Robert Tornello won the International Motorsports Association (IMSA) championship beating 84 drivers. During his IMSA racing years, Robert drove a Lola with a Chevrolet power plant and a Porsche 935 prototype. For him, 200 mph was a "comfortable speed.

"We all thought ourselves to be invincible," Robert says. Then a friend of his was killed, another was crippled, and he gave up racing professionally to become a farmer. The father of three young boys—Giancarlo, Dante and Angelo—Robert named his Ruskin, Fla., hydroponic farm after them. 3 Boys Farm is an award-winning, sustainably designed farm like no other where Robert uses the same drive, ingenuity and quick thinking he used while racing to produce the hydroponic, pesticide-free lettuce, tomatoes and basil that are served at Raglan Road.

"We are the first true, organic hydroponic facility like this to be built in the U.S.A.," he says. Hydroponics is the science of growing plants in water rather than soil by adding mineral nutrients. "We grow our produce all year round—12 months of the year—which is unique for Florida." The 10-acre farm grows 12 varieties of leafy greens and five types of herbs. "We grow heirloom tomatoes, cucumbers, peppers and eggplants. We do potatoes all year round, but the vine crops we do off-season when nobody locally can produce them."

At 3 Boys Farm everything is truly organic and sustainable. Up to 60 percent of the farm's energy needs are supplied by sun and wind. "We have 10 kilowatts of solar and 2 kilowatts of wind power, but that will increase," Robert explains. "We are just getting ready to install solar fans, which will take care of the cooling that we need." The farm does not produce waste or emissions, and the air that gets released from the greenhouses has a higher level of oxygen in it than the air that comes in. "Most greenhouses would use 12,000 to 15,000 gallons of water per day to water their crops," Robert says. "At 3 Boys we use only 500 gallons. We re-use and recycle. We've won a lot of agricultural awards."

The farm does not use pesticides but instead uses natural predators to control pests. The predators are beneficial insects like lacewings, which go after aphids. The farm also releases spider mites every six weeks to control pests. For his tomatoes, Robert has installed an in-house bumblebee hive to provide pollinators for the plants.

Racing prototype cars at 200 mph aside, Robert's background is in botany and landscape architecture. He once grew plants at the farm for zoos and theme parks and shipped them all over the world. The plants went into habitats for animals such as pandas and gorillas, so they had to be organic. Business was good until the economy took a massive shift.

Suddenly, Robert faced a big challenge. "What was I going do with 20 employees so that I didn't have to lay them off?" Despite the doubts of many, he decided to build his state-of- the-art produce farm, sinking an additional $3 million into the place to begin organic food production.

"This type of farming is very capital-intensive up front," Robert explains. "Everything is built to last at least 50 years here for true sustainability. It can't be blown down, there's nothing that will rot, decay or burn." The only things that need attention are the special polycarbonates on his greenhouse roofs, which need to be changed every 15 years.

Farming was never foreign to the Tornello family. Robert's father's family had farms in Sicily and a catering business in New York. His mother's family was from Naples, Italy, where they were in agriculture, too. But Robert's decision to farm hydroponic produce brought a challenge—taste. Many chefs will not touch hydroponic produce because they believe it has no real flavour.

Robert explains that many hydroponic foods are grown using chemical fertilizers and additives like high-nitrate salts. "The plants grow and get colour, but there is no cell wall strength... and there really is no taste. It's like eating a tasteless green fiber."

By farming organically, avoiding chemicals and allowing the plants to dictate the PH, Robert's plants offer great taste.

"We make natural, organic fertilizers ourselves in a process that's similar to brewing in a microbrewery. We start with pure organic sugarcane molasses, and then we add our nutrients to it. We brew it and cool it three times," says Robert. It sounds like a process that Guinness itself might applaud. Thanks to the sugar in the molasses, the stalks on 3 Boys' Romaine lettuce have sweet, great flavor, rather than bitterness. "We have created a liquid earth," he says. "Every chef who eats our product wants it in his kitchen."

Robert has strong views on cheap produce sourced through distributors in central Florida. "They bring in a lot of stuff from Peru and Chile, and it's laced with pesticides, some of which might be banned in the U.S. You can't wash that off. It's in the cell wall of the plant. Produce might be seven-to-10 days old by the time it gets to your shopping basket. Ours is 24 hours old, and we ship it with the root tube on so it's still a living organism when you get it. When people taste it, it changes their whole world."

Robert is also working with new Haitian farmers, men in their mid-to-late 40s who are just learning how to farm even though previous generations farmed before them. "So I asked them, 'Why did you never learn to farm if your grandfathers and fathers farmed?'" A mix of cheap imported food and free food from aid programmes played their part to badly impact Haitian agriculture. Though a generation of farmers was lost, they now are learning how to farm sustainably. Robert is happy to teach them how to grow non-tropical crops like lettuce in tropical or high-salt areas.

Always a risk taker, Robert has succeeded in farming fresh, tasty produce all year round without harming the earth's resources and while preserving the land for his three boys for years to come.

We have seen how the brewing process works for Guinness and for Robert's hydroponic farm, but there is another natural process that produces one of our daily necessities. The road to Raglan Road now stops at a bakery in Orlando, Florida, that supplies bread to the pub and restaurant. We also learn the curious tale of the 16-year-old who contributes a part of everything they bake.

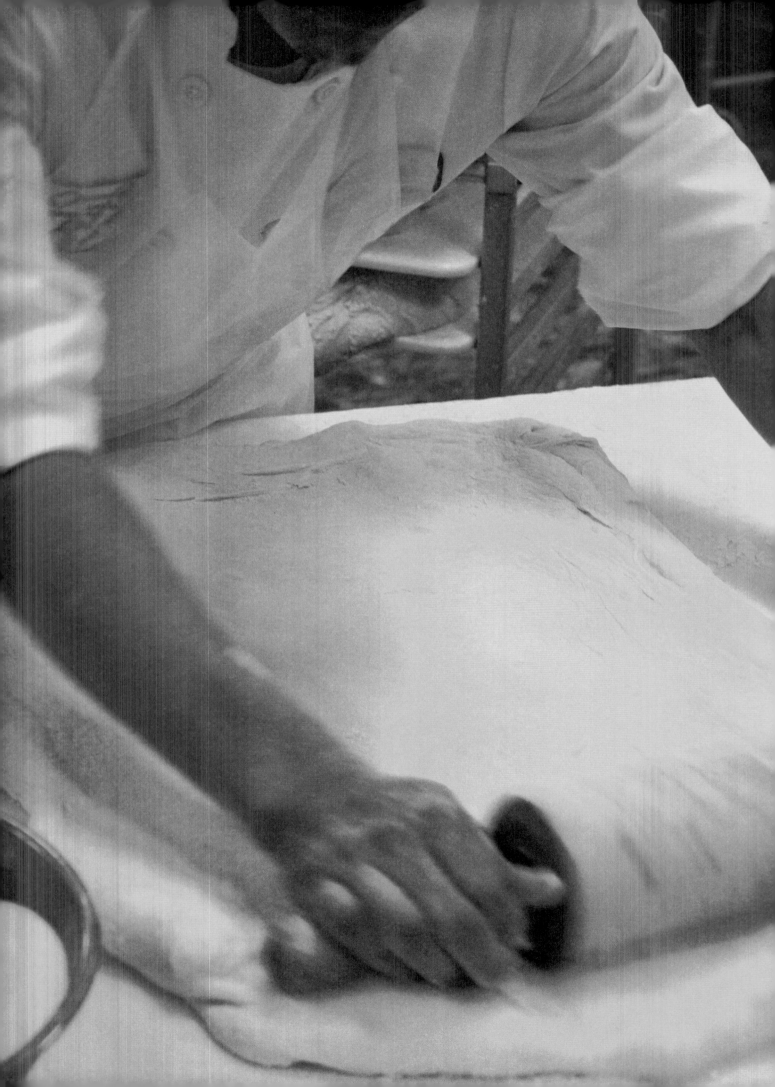

MOTHER DOUGH

Business Park Boulevard, Winter Garden, Florida, USA.
Sophie Sacagiu: 'Douce France' Bakery

Sophie Sacagiu was born in the town of Alençon in Normandy, France. Although she left Normandy for America when she was only 12, she retains strong memories—especially of the food—of her homeland. She recalls breaking the ends off crusty baguettes bought at the local bakery. She remembers the butter, the apples, the yoghurt, and especially the cheese from the rich farming region that produces Camembert, Livarot, Pont l'Eveque and Boursin (her mother was born just outside the town that gives Livarot cheese its name). Above all, she recalls that everything was natural and fresh.

"Everything that they call organic right now was just normal back then in France," Sophie says. That same commitment to top-quality, natural ingredients is evident at Douce France, the bakery she now runs with her husband Ran.

Sophie and Ran started the bakery almost 17 years ago in the city of Winter Garden, Fla., located on the edge of Orlando.

"My father had a prestigious French restaurant, 'La Normandie,' and he was in need of good bread," Sophie says. The family tested the market in the Orlando area but could not find the quality of bread they were looking for, so Sophie and Ran took the significant step of opening their own bakery. They first baked French, German and Italian breads, then breakfast pastries, and soon they began supplying local restaurants, including Raglan Road.

The bakery uses only the finest ingredients. "The main thing is to have high-quality, clean flour which is free of bromides," Sophie says. Douce France Bakery has flour milled specifically for them in Indiantown, Fla., using only premium wheat. They use a mix of spring and winter flour. "Winter flour has less protein, which gives the bread more body and flavor," Sophie explains. To the flour, they add top-grade Wisconsin butter. Though they produce a high volume of bread, Douce France remains an artisan bakery where the dough and artisan breads are still made by hand instead of machine.

"The most important ingredient that goes into our bread is time," says Sophie. Their sourdough is 16 years old and forms the basis of all their bread. "It's the mother dough. We nourish it twice a day. It may sound weird but it's priceless." This type of mother dough is called a "levain" in French, and its natural enzymes work to produce the flavours in the bread. "Any kind of French bread with crustiness cannot be made overnight—it has to be made with a heavy dough that has been fermented. We take a little bit of our mother dough, depending on the recipe and work it into the new dough to give it a lot of flavour and consistency." Many other bakeries create their dough with mixes that may include ingredients like vinegar, but Douce France dough is completely natural.

"Bread is a living thing," she says. The mother dough is left in the cooler and fed twice a day by adding more flour and more water. "A little too much water or a little too much flour and the dough dies," Sophie says. Thanks to the mother dough, Douce France can use less yeast than other bakeries.

To keep in touch with new recipes and trends in the marketplace, the bakery calls on consultant Didier Rosada, one of the top American bread makers. He was the unofficial trainer of Baking Team USA that finished first in the bread category at the "Coupe de Monde de Boulangerie" in Paris in 1996. Rosada has advised Douce France on making bread completely trans-fat free. "His insights help us to stay more consistent and keep the quality of our bread high," says Sophie.

From the French outpost of Douce France Bakery, our next step on the road to Raglan Road takes us back to the streets of Dublin where the pungent and mouthwatering smell of fish and chips is in the (slightly damp and chilly) air.

Index

Talk to you soon...